An Illustrated History of
Eastleigh
Locomotive Works

In February 1967, Bo-Bo electro-diesel locomotive No E6018 undergoes its first intermediate overhaul and is supported on stands over a pit in the erecting shop at Eastleigh. The use of electro-diesel locomotives on British Rail Southern Region was unique in Britain. On the E6000 series locomotives (later TOPS Class 73), retractable shoes were provided on each bogie for conductor rail current collection. This was the normal mode of operation on main lines by which means a locomotive could exert 1,600bhp.

When taking freight trains to or from yards that did not have the third rail, the driver was able to start the 600bhp English Electric 4SRKT engine, lift up the collector shoes, and drive under diesel power. At different times the class was overhauled at both Crewe and Eastleigh works. (The extended cab yellow on No E6018 did not please the SR general manager of the day and was quietly abandoned then, but the style reappeared many years later during BR's business management era.) *Colin Boocock*

This panoramic view of Eastleigh Locomotive Works was photographed from the end of the main office block roof in April 1960. Even as late as the second half of the 20th century, some ancient former LSWR steam locomotives like the Adams 'radial' tanks were still receiving general overhauls. No 30582 of this type stands in the front of the works yard receiving last-minute attention prior to its release to traffic for the Lyme Regis branch.

In the left background the four hipped roofs of the works' erecting shop bays can be clearly seen, while in the centre is the lower section roof with 'north lights' covering the fitting and machine shops. To the far right is the foundry block.

The row of five narrow chimneys behind that building identifies the position of the boilers feeding the forge hammers. In front of the erecting shop, extreme left, a Maunsell 'S15' class 4-6-0 undergoes post-overhaul steam tests. On its right are a BR Standard Class 3 2-6-2T, alongside the safety valve test building, and diesel shunting locomotives which are already beginning to appear for works attention. Rows of locomotives of LSWR, SR and BR origin are on the right of the picture, awaiting their turn to be shunted into the erecting shop for attention. An 'M7' 0-4-4T acts as yard shunting locomotive, right. *Colin Boocock*

An Illustrated History of
Eastleigh
Locomotive Works

Colin Boocock and Peter Stanton

An imprint of
Ian Allan Publishing

First published 2006

ISBN (10) 0 86093 605 8
ISBN (13) 978 0 86093 605 3

© Colin Boocock and Peter Stanton 2006

Published by Oxford Publishing Co

an imprint of Ian Allan Publishing Ltd, Hersham, Surrey KT12 4RG. Printed in England by Ian Allan Printing Ltd, Hersham, Surrey KT12 4RG.

Code: 0608/B1

Visit the Ian Allan Publishing website at www.ianallanpublishing.com

Dedication

This book is dedicated to all the men and women of all professions, skills and ranks who have worked on the Eastleigh Locomotive Works site at any time between the construction of the works in the early 20th century and its closure in 2006. They made it the fascinating and successful place that it was and they gladly shared with all new employees the huge volume of knowledge and experience that was generated there.

Contents

Right: **BR Standard Class 3 2-6-2T No 82016 has been delivered by Eastleigh Locomotive Works to the nearby running shed following overhaul in late 1958, and needs a live steam injector cap tightening to complete its readiness for service. Works fitter Eddie Paine applies the necessary leverage.** *Tony Brown*

Introduction

Above: **Eastleigh Locomotive Works erecting shop in late LSWR days was normally a place of intense activity. In this view, locomotives of Adams, Drummond and Urie designs are in different stages of overhaul or repair. A set of frames for a new 4-6-0 locomotive stands on the right ready for its frame stretchers to be added and riveted in place. On the left is a pair of large diameter driving wheels for an inside-cylinder 4-4-0, showing the two heavy cranks that made failure-free crank axle design such a challenge. In later years, components such as the leaf springs and brackets that are seen lying about here haphazardly were more tidily held in large steel trays. Also, the wooden plank floor was replaced in Southern Railway years by wood block flooring, which lasted well into the British Railways period.** *Hampshire Museums Service*

Eastleigh Locomotive Works has an important place in British railway history for several reasons. It was the last of the big workshops built by a major railway company for the construction and overhaul of its locomotives, being opened in 1909. It built some very interesting and successful steam locomotives, particularly under Southern Railway ownership. Apart from raw materials purchases, Eastleigh's engineering was almost fully self-supporting during the steam era. It played a significant part in the 1939-1945 war effort and later became a major overhaul facility for Southern Region diesel and electric traction.

Eastleigh Locomotive Works was capable of embracing enormous, fundamental changes, as was seen in 1967 when the larger carriage works nearby moved into space inside the smaller locomotive works without reducing its output of carriage overhauls. Since then Eastleigh has played its part in the changes that privatisation brought to the railways of Britain although it eventually had to succumb to market forces. Modern carriages needed fewer overhauls and the works' capacity was no longer needed by its last owners. Alstom closed the site in 2006, thereby denying us all the pleasure of celebrating the centenary of Eastleigh Locomotive Works by just three years.

The London & South Western Railway had built 814* locomotives at its Nine Elms Works in London, up until 1908. Moving this work into the larger plant at Eastleigh enabled bigger and better locomotives to be constructed and attention to be given to the overhaul of the rest of the ever-expanding fleet. The locomotive works at Eastleigh eventually produced 314 new steam locomotives and substantially rebuilt 115. Even so, its greater work volume was in the overhaul and repair of locomotives and the provision of components for the LSWR, the Southern Railway (a duty shared with works at Ashford and Brighton), and British Railways. Within BR it specialised in supporting the Southern Region fleet, although not exclusively, and not just the steam locomotives either.

After absorbing the work of the nearby carriage works in 1967, Eastleigh Works' emphasis began to swing away from locomotives towards passenger carriages, particularly multiple-units, and also parcels vans and containers. The works became part of British Rail Maintenance Limited (BRML) in 1988 until privatised in 1995, becoming Wessex Traincare Limited as the result of a management buyout. The international train-builder GEC-Alsthom (later renamed Alstom) bought the company and the works in 1998. However, early in the 21st century, the train operating company South West Trains awarded its major EMU replacement contract to Siemens and not to Alstom. The subsequent setting up of Siemens' own

*The 814 locomotives built at Nine Elms Works included the engines and under-frames of 17 steam railcars that were then sent to Eastleigh Carriage Works for fitting with carriage bodies.

Above: Among the many skills specific to the boilermakers' trade was that of expanding flue tubes so that they fitted tightly in the firebox and smokebox tubeplates. In this view, an expanding tool is being used to make a Maunsell 4-6-0 locomotive boiler with three-row superheater properly water and steam tight. The Southern disapproved of those railways that permitted tubes to be welded in position, insisting that tube expanding was sufficient when done properly. *Hampshire Museums Service*

Left: New cast-iron components such as brake blocks and even chairs for railway tracks were made in quantity on Eastleigh's specialised casting plant. This was situated in one corner of the iron foundry, where a continuous belt carried sand moulds round an elongated circuit, the molten iron being poured into the moulds from ladles carried by hoists. The iron cooled in the moulds as they proceeded around the circuit to a point on the opposite side, where the moulds were broken open and the castings removed. These were then sent to an annexe for fettling, namely to have the rough edges and flashes removed by air-operated power chisels. *Hampshire Museums Service*

Right: The most powerful and arguably the most successful locomotives to be built and later overhauled and then rebuilt at Eastleigh Locomotive Works were the Bulleid 'Merchant Navy' class Pacifics. Some time around the end of World War 2, No 21C1 *Channel Packet* hangs from two 60-ton overhead Vaughan cranes over a side pit in the erecting shop. One of the new members of the class is near completion in the adjacent bay (left of the columns) and a Drummond 'M7' 0-4-4T stands on the right-side pit track (or 'pit road' in local parlance). *Hampshire Museums Service*

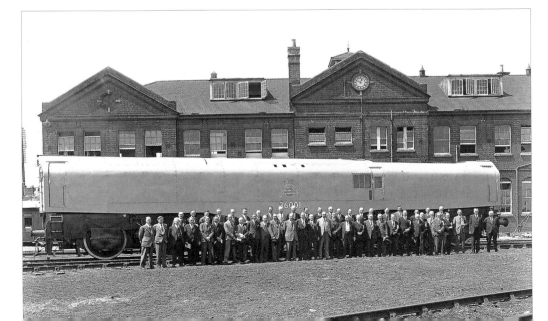

Left: Although not built at Eastleigh, the first Bulleid 'Leader' class 0-6-6-0T No 36001 did appear there for trials and modifications, and indeed was eventually dismantled there. It was at Eastleigh on the occasion of a visit by the Institution of Mechanical Engineers in August 1950. Works Manager K. H. Morriss is on the extreme right of this photograph posed outside the works offices. *Ian Allan Library*

depot at Northam, Southampton, robbed Eastleigh of the potential for any significant future overhaul work. Eastleigh's last duties were overhauls of some Gatwick Express Class 460 units and refurbishments of Merseyrail Class 507/508s and Southern Class 455 suburban EMUs. Alstom announced the closure of Eastleigh Works which took place on 31 March 2006.

Author Colin Boocock enjoyed his engineering apprenticeship at Eastleigh Locomotive Works (1954 to 1959). He spent some time in the drawing office (1959 to 1961) and took the opportunity later, to work there in management (1965 to 1969). His experiences at Eastleigh enhance the content of this book, reducing substantially the amount of second-hand information needed to bring this history to life. Peter Stanton's career also took him to Eastleigh as the Southern Region's Area Electrification & Plant Engineer, South Western (1985 to 1989).

The authors are grateful to many people and organisations for access to the photographs and other illustrations used in this book, and for permission to publish them. They also thank friends and colleagues who provided information. This book comes at a sad time, following the closure of Eastleigh Works early in 2006. Life, however, goes on, and it is good to have something to help recall memories of interesting times. We hope this book will do that for many people.

Colin Boocock
Peter Stanton

Right: **A major task undertaken at Eastleigh in the later 1950s and early 1960s was to rebuild all 30 'Merchant Navy' 4-6-2s and 60 of the 110 Bulleid light Pacifics. This rebuilding replaced the Bulleid valve gear by three independent sets of Walschaerts gear, incorporated a new inside cylinder and frame stretcher, and a new, longer smokebox and cast chimney and petticoat to improve combustion. The semi-streamlined cladding was replaced by conventional boiler lagging plates and side valances. The excellent boiler was retained virtually unmodified, apart from repositioning the safety valves further back. The rebuilt locomotives continued to perform well and were significantly more economical to operate than before rebuilding. Here, 'Battle of Britain' 4-6-2 No 34082 *615 Squadron* is being lowered on to its coupled wheels in the erecting shop on 14 April 1960.** *Colin Boocock*

Left: **Even as late as 1964 some old locomotives were still being overhauled in the erecting shop. In this view of No 4 bay, a Stroudley 'Terrier' 0-6-0T and a row of tenders from Bulleid Pacifics receive attention.** *British Railways*

Above: **Type 3 BRCW/Sulzer Bo-Bo diesel-electric No D6558 stands inside the new diesel test house in 1966. This was provided as part of the 1962 Workshops Plan when Eastleigh Locomotive Works had been designated as an on-going works. The locomotive's generator was coupled electrically to resistance load banks so that the engine could be run in and** tested under controlled rotation speeds to full output. *Colin Boocock*

Below: **Bo-Bo dc electric No E5004 is seen in the works yard at Eastleigh on 10 September 1959. This locomotive was visiting for unscheduled repair at that time.** *Colin Boocock*

Above: **This aerial view looking south-east shows the full extent of the combined Eastleigh Works site in the BREL/BRML era. The main line is in the foreground, the Portsmouth line to the left of the site, and the single track in the far distance connects to the rear of the running shed area. The main works buildings are distinguished by the four long bays with clearance for lifting vehicles. The lower-roofed section in the centre contained the** machine and ancillary shops. The former foundry block with its two hipped roofs is on the right of the site. In the foreground, the constricted approach road over Campbell Road bridge is obvious: the sharpest corners have been relieved to permit articulated lorries to reach the works. The tracks on the extreme left of the picture lead into the site of the former carriage works, now an industrial estate. *Nigel Guppy collection*

Right: **The last major contract that Eastleigh Works had, under Alstom ownership, was to refurbish Class 455 EMUs on lease to the train operator Southern, as seen in this view of the main carriage shop on 19 July 2005. Because modern units require fewer overhauls, Eastleigh Works needed to gain some useful contracts with 'half-life' work such as this in order to remain in business. With an absence of any follow-on contracts, the works was due to close at the end of this programme, early in 2006.** *Colin Boocock*

Acknowledgements

The authors thank wholeheartedly all who have helped by adding information and illustrations to make this book as complete as it is. We make special mention of Wendy Bowen (Hampshire County Council Museums and Archives Service), Sarah Canham (National Railway Museum), Nigel Guppy (Alstom), Brian Morrison (photographer), Malcolm Stainthorpe (past Eastleigh Works manager), and Peter Waller (for access to the Ian Allan Library), all of whose efforts are gratefully acknowledged.

Bibliography

Readers of this illustrated history of Eastleigh Locomotive Works may find the following books of interest. They proved really useful to the authors and are recommended for further reading on this subject.

War on the Line — The Southern Railway in Wartime by Bernard Darwin, published by the Southern Railway Company, 1946. Written in somewhat flamboyant style, this small book nonetheless contains information and emotion that will touch the heart of anyone who remembers World War 2 and will be an eye-opener for anyone too young to know what actually went on at that time.

LSWR Locomotives by F. Burtt, published by Ian Allan Ltd, 1949. This well-researched book contains lists with building and rebuilding dates of all locomotives ever owned by the LSWR and gives descriptions, dimensional details and illustrations of most classes and major variations.

Built at Eastleigh (Revised Edition), An Illustrated List of Steam Locomotives Built or Rebuilt 1910-1961 by Eric Forge, edited by Gavin Bowie with research by Colin Asprey, published by Waterfront Publications, 1992, ISBN 0 946184 17 8. This is a complete record of all steam locomotives built at Eastleigh Locomotive Works. Well illustrated.

The LSWR at Nine Elms, The Curl Collection Volume 1, The Works and its Products by Barry Curl, published by KRB Publications, 2004, ISBN 0 954203 57 7. Based on a unique collection of photographs and archives rescued from Eastleigh, this book is the definitive volume on Nine Elms Works. The illustrations alone make this an essential part of any LSWR book collection. This is history writ well!

The first three of these books are available from time to time on the second-hand market, which the authors have successfully accessed through Amazon.co.uk. The Nine Elms book is available from its publisher and through all good book shops and internet book stores.

Glossary

It is useful to explain the meanings of certain technical terms that might be misunderstood, particularly as some words are used in the railway world with different meanings in different areas. At Eastleigh as well as elsewhere, the word **repair**, for example, was often used when the word **overhaul** would have been more appropriate, and which has become modern parlance. The key definitions that the authors prefer to use for the main activities at Eastleigh are as follows:

Build/construct: The assembly of a new locomotive using new components.

Rebuild: Engineering change to an existing locomotive that alters its design in one or more substantial ways.

Repair: Making good by engineering methods a damaged or non-performing component or locomotive.

Overhaul: Dismantling, repairing where necessary and reassembling a locomotive or major component with new, repaired or overhauled components.

General overhaul: An overhaul that affects all components of a locomotive. It includes a complete locomotive repaint.

Intermediate overhaul: An overhaul that affects the running gear, such as wheels, cylinders, bogies, traction motors and power unit, but which excludes lifting the boiler from the frames. Repainting may be done, but the practice on steam locomotives was normally just to touch up and revarnish the existing paintwork.

Casual overhaul: An overhaul of specific components such as steam locomotive valves and pistons, or unscheduled tyre re-profiling.

The star locomotives of the steam fleets that were overhauled by Eastleigh Locomotive Works were undoubtedly the rebuilt 'Merchant Navy' class 4-6-2s. On 1 February 1959, No 35017 *Belgian Marine* was photographed in full cry ascending Pokesdown bank with the heavy 'Bournemouth Belle' Pullman train. A regular feature of LSWR and Southern Railway steam locomotives using good-quality Kent steam coal was the lack of black smoke. *Colin Boocock*

1. The Nine Elms legacy

The London & South Western Railway built its original locomotive works at Nine Elms in London, opening it for locomotive attention in 1839. This was on a site on the north side of the railway in the area of the former Nine Elms market gardens. Steam locomotive construction began there in 1842, but by the early 1860s expansion of the LSWR had led to a need for a larger facility. Thus, from 1865, new works facilities were progressively built on the south side of the railway. The former works site was transferred to the operating department and became a

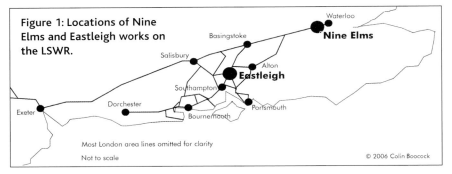

Figure 1: Locations of Nine Elms and Eastleigh works on the LSWR.

Most London area lines omitted for clarity

Not to scale

© 2006 Colin Boocock

Below: **The need for a new locomotive works on the LSWR became evident as Nine Elms Locomotive Works became more crowded. This picture is of the machine shop at Nine Elms in October 1904 and shows almost no spare floor space. Axleboxes, connecting rods and coupling rods are piled high and there is copious white metal swarf on the ground. Indeed, the conditions there would now be regarded as unsafe under modern industrial standards. The narrow gauge track running through the gangway is part of the works' system for transporting components from shop to shop.**
Nigel Guppy collection

large goods handling yard and depot. The new Nine Elms Works began building locomotives around 1873, but further pressure on capacity was met by another expansion of the works on the new site, which was completed by 1878. The site also included an enlarged locomotive depot in the form of a semi-roundhouse. A later depot, the one that older, present-generation railway enthusiasts may remember, was built on part of the site at Nine Elms that was relinquished after the works had been moved to Eastleigh in 1909.

By the end of the 19th century, the requirements for locomotive building and overhauls were once again outstripping the works at Nine Elms. The LSWR looked for a greenfield site on which to build a much larger, modern locomotive works and chose to use land near the village of Bishopstoke, north of Southampton. A new carriage and wagon works had already been established nearby and subsequently the town of Eastleigh grew up largely as a result of the railway activity in the area.

Among locomotives built at Nine Elms Works were many of the products of the two Beatties (father and son), William Adams and Dugald Drummond, all locomotive

Above: **The machines in Nine Elms machine shop were driven by belts, themselves powered in turn by the long shafts that threaded the sides of the shop. These were driven originally by stationary steam engines and the belt drives were hazardous to staff who could lose limbs or scalps if they carelessly got too close to them. Among the clutter of overhead shafts, belts and compressed air lines there is no evidence of provision of any form of artificial lighting — the natural light from the roof glazing was all they had! Imagine working in this crowded scene on a dismal winter's afternoon.** *Courtesy National Railway Museum*

superintendents of the LSWR. These were typical locomotives of the period, mainly 0-6-0 goods engines, 2-4-0, 0-4-2, 4-4-0 and 0-4-4T passenger classes, and a few 0-4-0T and 0-6-0T shunting engines. Drummond, however, had an adventurous streak and produced some four-cylinder express locomotives with uncoupled driving wheels with an unusual 4-2-2-0 wheel arrangement. His 4-4-0s were more successful than these, and legendary classes such as the 'T9' 'Greyhounds' and the big 'D15s' ran heavy express trains for decades on the Bournemouth

and Portsmouth lines. Drummond's big 4-6-0s were also unusual, this time because they used four cylinders, high pitched boilers, and there were probably insufficient means of distributing and using the very low-superheat steam. The 4-6-0s apparently did no better work than his 4-4-0s, and were a burden landed on Eastleigh Locomotive Works when that place was called on by Chief Mechanical Engineer Robert Urie to rebuild them into more useful machines.

Among the locomotives used for London suburban work out of Waterloo station were the Beattie well tanks, many of which had been rebuilt from 2-4-0 tender engines. These small machines were sprightly performers and were successful until train loads became greater. To cope with heavier loads, Adams developed his delightful 'O2' class 0-4-4Ts, some later becoming famous for being the staple motive power on the Isle of Wight from the 1930s right through to electrification in 1966. The 'T1' class was a larger development, but Drummond's main work on this type was the 'M7' class 0-4-4T which survived in quantity on Southern lines until 1964, just three years before the end of SR steam.

So when Eastleigh Locomotive Works opened for business in 1909 it faced the overhaul of a mixed and varied fleet of locomotives, as well as the need to improve them and to construct new, larger engines to enable the advance of the LSWR and the Southern Railway and British Railways after it.

Class codes

In this chapter we have been referring to LSWR locomotive class designations such as 'M7' and 'T9' without explaining what they mean for the uninitiated. In fact, these codes do not themselves convey any particular information about the locomotives, their size, wheel arrange-

ment or their power. Each designation applied was simply the order number placed on the works for the first locomotive or batch of locomotives constructed of that class. Thus order number 'B4' placed on Nine Elms Works was for some 0-4-0Ts for service in the company's docks. Order No S14 was for the first locomotive built at Eastleigh Locomotive Works. Indeed, the order number ranges 14, 15 and 16 occupied Eastleigh right up to the time of the Grouping in 1923, following which completely new SR locomotive designs were given code letters similar to the Maunsell classes that had emerged from Ashford works (e.g. 'Q' class 0-6-0, 'V' class 4-4-0 and 'W' class 2-6-4T), but which still gave no clue about each class's characteristics. But then, the 'Lord Nelson' class became Class LN, precipitating a different code

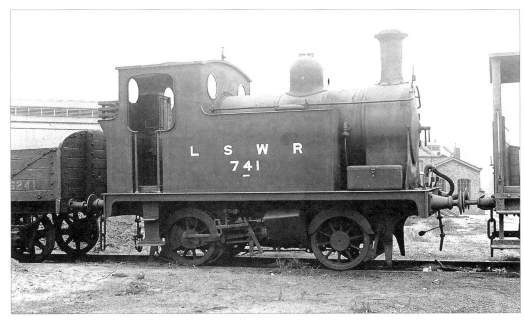

Right: A small product from Nine Elms Locomotive Works was a group of tiny 2-2-0Ts designed by Drummond for single-carriage push-pull or 'motor' trains. No 741 of Class C14 was built there in 1906. The short white line under the running number in this photograph, taken at Strawberry Hill on 24 September 1921, indicates that the locomotive had been transferred to the duplicate list, that is taken off capital stock, although still operational. *W. Beckerlegge*

Left: To enable him to get about the LSWR system quickly, Dugald Drummond designed and had built at Nine Elms in 1899, this pleasantly proportioned 4-2-4T steam carriage No 733, known affectionately in some quarters as 'Drummond's bug'. Around the time of the closure of Nine Elms Works in 1909, Drummond used this engine on frequent visits to Eastleigh as the building of the new works there progressed. He continued to travel in it almost daily from Surbiton to Eastleigh and back when Eastleigh Locomotive Works was in full production.

It may be an apocryphal tale, but it was said that Drummond spent as much time on these journeys in the driving cab as in his special saloon! After the unit was dismantled in 1940, the carriage portion was used for many years as a hut in Eastleigh Locomotive Works yard while the frames, without the driving axle, served to transport heavy loads around the works yard. *Bucknall collection/Ian Allan Library*

philosophy that was to be followed by 'MN' for the 'Merchant Navy' class, and 'WC' and 'BB' for the 'West Country'/'Battle of Britain' class. Presumably, the 'Schools' class 4-4-0s (Class V) escaped being known as Class S because a solitary ex-South Eastern & Chatham Railway 0-6-0 saddle tank had already been allocated that designation.

When the London, Brighton & South Coast Railway rebuilt a locomotive it usually added the letter 'X' to the class code. For example, when Brighton Works super-heated the Stroudley 'A1' class 0-6-0Ts they became Class A1X. The SR added the letter 'R' when some Class E1 0-6-0Ts were rebuilt into 0-6-2Ts, becoming Class E1/R. The odd one in this group was the use of Class N15X to describe the rebuilding at Eastleigh of the former LBSCR Billinton Class L 4-6-4Ts into the 'Remembrance' class 4-6-0s. From their new code one would assume they were rebuilds of Class N15 ('King Arthur') 4-6-0s, but they

Above: A characteristic class of the Adams era was the pretty 0-4-2 tender engine design, the 'A12', intended for secondary passenger workings. No 608 was delivered to the LSWR in 1892 by Neilson. A few of this class were extant in British Railways days, just. All received their overhauls, first at Nine Elms then at Eastleigh Locomotive Works.
Bucknall collection/Ian Allan Library

Below: Drummond's classic express 4-4-0 design was the Class T9 of which 66 examples were built, many at Nine Elms, but those numbered from 702 upwards were supplied by Dübs. In its original unsuperheated state, and with cross-firebox water tubes, Nine Elms-built No 303 heads west on the main line near Earlsfield with a down Bournemouth express.
F. Moore's Railway Photographs/Bucknall collection/Ian Allan Library

Above: **Among locomotives built at Nine Elms were many 2-4-0 tender engines, some of which were later rebuilt there to form suburban tank engines. The last locomotives to survive from the Beattie stable were three of these 2-4-0 well tanks. These outlived their compatriots by decades due to their usefulness on the lightly laid Wenford Bridge freight branch in Cornwall. No 30586 stands at Eastleigh depot on 2 March 1960 after its last general overhaul in the locomotive works. Two of these locomotives are now preserved.** *Colin Boocock*

Below: **William Adams produced and maintained at Nine Elms Works the successful Class O2 0-4-4Ts that were initially applied to suburban workings around London. They later dispersed to local services and branch lines at the extremities of the system, including several that gave stalwart service on the Isle of Wight from the 1930s through to electrification in 1966. One of these is preserved at Havenstreet. This picture shows No 30225 after general overhaul at Eastleigh, on 28 April 1959.** *Colin Boocock*

were not of course. They were, however, in the same power and performance class, and were intended for the South Western Section, so the new code may just have been to appease the operating department.

Locomotives that had been built for the LSWR by outside contractors were classified by the number of the first locomotive. Thus the Drummond freight 0-6-0s were always known as the '700' class, which was the number of the first locomotive of the class delivered to the LSWR by Dübs.

Right: In attempting to develop larger express passenger engines, Dugald Drummond first opted for four cylinders and an uncoupled layout for the driving wheels. His Class T6 4-2-2-0 No 720 was built at Nine Elms in 1897. The uncoupled wheels idea was not entirely successful, with less effective adhesion, and Drummond went on to design simpler, two-cylinder 4-4-0s that performed very well indeed. *Bucknall collection/Ian Allan Library*

Middle: The Class F13 and G14 four-cylinder 4-6-0s and other similar types were not among the best of Mr Drummond's large engines and it fell to Eastleigh Works to rebuild these locomotives under Robert Urie's direction. The 'F13s', including No 330 depicted, were small-wheeled 4-6-0s, had four cylinders and were intended for freight and West of England passenger trains. They were apparently the earliest standard gauge locomotives in Britain to have outside Walschaerts valve gear to the outside cylinders. This was not their Achilles' heel, however, but there was probably a serious mismatch between the boiler and steam distribution arrangements to feed the four cylinders. Mr Urie had them rebuilt at Eastleigh into simple, two-cylinder machines with better, but not startling results. *Bucknall collection/Ian Allan Library*

Below: Built at Nine Elms in 1908, 'G14' No 457 is moving well along the main line near Earlsfield with an up express. It was some years away from the time when its rebuilding into a new 'King Arthur' 4-6-0 was to take place. *Bucknall collection/Ian Allan Library*

Above: As the works ran down at Nine Elms and sections were transferred to the new locomotive works at Eastleigh, some shops became ghost areas. This is the wheel shop with a few old wheel lathes still in position but the rest of activity and equipment has already departed. *Nigel Guppy collection*

Below: The end has come and demolition is under way at Nine Elms Locomotive Works. Two workers look glumly at the remains and contemplate the task of removing heavy equipment. Beyond the rubble, through the doorway, can be seen one of the old forge steam hammers. *Nigel Guppy collection*

2. The new Eastleigh Locomotive Works

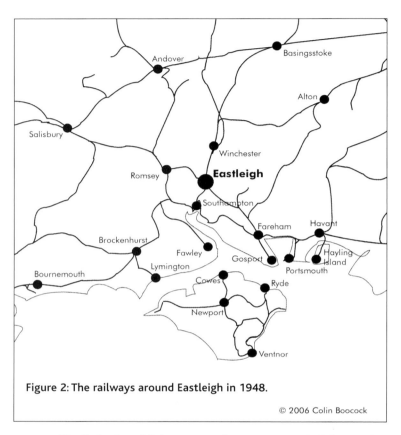

Figure 2: The railways around Eastleigh in 1948.

© 2006 Colin Boocock

Until the late 19th century the area around Bishopstoke, situated six miles north-east of Southampton, was mainly flat farmland. The London & Southampton Railway's main line passed through the area in a generally north-east/south-west direction. Junctions had been laid there for new secondary routes to link the main line with Gosport to the south, and Salisbury to the north-west. The junction station was originally called Bishopstoke, but later it became Eastleigh & Bishopstoke, and only from 1923 did it become just Eastleigh, these changes reflecting the growth of the town of this name.

In 1894, the London & South Western Railway had succeeded in moving its carriage building and overhaul workshops from Nine Elms to a greenfield site alongside the main and Gosport lines at Bishopstoke. The following year, Dugald Drummond was appointed Locomotive Superintendent of the LSWR, and in 1905, his post was redesignated Chief Mechanical Engineer. Drummond could see a pressing need for improved facilities for

building and overhauling the railway's locomotive fleet. There were about 50 acres of flat space in the fork of the junction between the Southampton and Bournemouth main line and the line to Gosport and Portsmouth and this was earmarked for the new locomotive works. Land alongside, nearer the main line, housed the large running sheds that had been opened in 1902.

Construction of the works progressed such that staff and equipment began to move there from Nine Elms during 1909. Locomotive construction started almost immediately, initially on a small scale, with two 0-4-0Ts outshopped late in 1910.

Mr Drummond stated at the time that Eastleigh Locomotive Works was 'the most complete and up-to-date works owned by any railway company'. We have no reason to doubt that. It was designed to enable nearly all components for locomotives to be manufactured on site. There were iron and brass foundries for producing castings, supported by a shop for making the wooden patterns used to form the sand moulds in the foundries. A forge with heavy-capacity steam hammers enabled steel billets to be formed into blanks for coupling and connecting rods, while a smith shop used smaller hammers to forge brake gear, spring hangers, drawgear and valve gear components and other stressed items. Machine and fitting shops changed these rough forgings or steel rods, strips and plates into identifiable components. A brass shop with machine and fitting staff overhauled and made new items in brass such as valves and pumps and included the assembly of complex items such as injectors. Few components were purchased from outside, apart from patented items such as vacuum brake ejectors and cylinders, Westinghouse air pumps for push-pull locomotives, and (later in the works' history) exhaust injectors for the economic feeding of water to boilers.

The boiler shop at the south-east end of the main workshop building had the capability of rolling and pressing steel and copper sheet into the shapes needed for boilers and fireboxes. Hydraulic presses for this work were fed with high-pressure water from a hydraulic ram outside the back of the works. In those days steam locomotive boilers were of riveted construction. It sounded like bedlam in the boiler shop as men worked power hammers to push red hot rivets home, and to seal boiler and firebox

seams and stay ends by caulking. Indeed, one of the results of all this noise was the almost inevitable deafness of the older boilermakers.

The main erecting shop and associated locomotive shops were located in four long and wide bays, each with three tracks. There were in total 67 pitted places on which locomotives could stand. New locomotive construction involved cutting plate frames to shape and then erecting them by riveting frame stretchers between them. A set of frames would then stand on its pit as the locomotive was assembled with its cylinders, boiler assembly and other principal components. It would later be lifted and placed on its coupled wheels, then lifted again so as to stand on a set of rollers for the valves to be set. After valve-setting the locomotive would be lifted once more to gain any extra carrying wheels. All lifts were undertaken by pairs of overhead cranes located in each shop bay. Locomotives would then be shunted to the paint shop so that painting could be carried out in relatively dust-free conditions. Overhauled locomotives followed a similar sequence.

Top: **The framework to support the first two bays of the four-bay erecting shop rises up alongside the Bishopstoke-Fareham railway line (out of sight to the left of this view). The runners for the heavy overhead cranes are already incorporated into the structures. Some of the building frames were transferred from the partially demolished Nine Elms Works.** *Hampshire Museums Service*

Above: **The frontage of the main buildings of Eastleigh Locomotive Works in the early Southern Railway period highlights the four hipped roofs of the erecting shop bays. Each bay has a central entrance doorway permitting locomotives to be shunted in and out. The lower building to the right has a north-light type of pitched roof in which the glazing is only on the north slope so that overheating from direct sunlight is minimised. The entrances to this building give access, left to right, to the fitting shop (two doorways), the stores, and what at that time was a separate shop for painting locomotives. (In later years the Southern Railway and British Railways painted locomotives in the erecting shop as they were reassembled.) Urie 'N15' 4-6-0 No 749 stands outside No 1 bay in the position of the steaming shed that was added later by the SR.** *Modern Transport/Ian Allan Library*

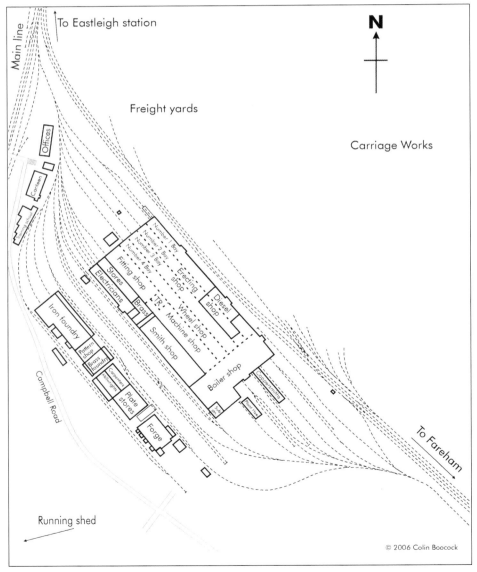

Above: **The foundry block dominates this view of part of the works in LSWR days. The iron foundry is by far the longest section of the block, occupying over half its length. Next to the iron foundry is the pattern shop in which wooden patterns for all types of castings were made, and beyond that is the relatively small brass foundry. The low lean-to building alongside the iron foundry was occupied by the casting fettlers, who used chisels (later mechanised) and grinders to chip off the risers and the excess metal flashes on castings.**

The fascinating selection of locomotives queuing up outside awaiting works attention includes, from left to right: Drummond 4-6-0 No 334, an Adams outside-cylinder express 4-4-0 behind which is a small 0-6-0ST; on the track between the main buildings is another, larger 0-6-0ST, behind the nearby lighting pole is an Adams 'radial' 4-4-2T without its boiler; and behind that on the adjacent track is one of the LSWR steam railcars. The LSWR had its locomotives facing the north-west exit of the works, but in 1931, the SR rearranged the system so that all locomotives faced south-east, and this remained the normal practice to the end of steam. *Bucknall collection/ Ian Allan Library*

Left: **Figure 3: Eastleigh Locomotive Works, 1960.**

In later years painting was done in the erecting shop, releasing shop space for other activities such as electrical repairs, and later still, the manufacture of plastic components.

The Ordnance Survey map of the area dated 1909, and an LSWR diagram of 1911, show the railway tracks in the works yard only extended north-west towards the main line. The 1933 map includes the full works track layout that extended behind as well as in front of the works. These tracks were useful to enable materials to be brought to the doors of the boiler shop and for equipment to be taken to and from the stores and other ancillary buildings. The power house provided the works with transformed and rectified electric power, and with hydraulic and compressed-air supplies for powering heavy machines and hand tools. Large motors at the end of each shop bay drove shafts which in turn drove the machinery in the works by long flat belts. Later changes brought individual, alternating current electric motor drives for each of the myriad of machines, eliminating most of the belt drives.

The forge and smith shop hammers were for many decades steam operated. The steam supply came from old

Above: **The main line through Eastleigh witnessed the passage of many very long freight trains to and from Southampton Docks. Here, Nine Elms-built Drummond Class F13 4-6-0 No 334 is seen on the down main line photographed from Campbell Road overbridge near the entrance to Eastleigh Locomotive Works. The track leading into the works is visible to the right, behind the wire fence. The two tracks between the works fence and the main line are the lines to and from the running sheds.** *Bucknall collection/Ian Allan Library*

Right: **Eastleigh erecting shop in LSWR days was a busy place. It was undoubtedly normally less tidy than seen in this specially posed official photograph which shows steam locomotives of Adams and Drummond origin in various stages of overhaul. The pair of radial wheels in the centre foreground has had its bearing surfaces carefully protected with bitumen grease. On the right is a pile of steel plate ashpans. There is no sign in this photograph of any artificial lighting. The roof glazing appears to have provided all the light by which men had to work, a difficult concept to imagine in the shorter days of winter.** *Courtesy National Railway Museum*

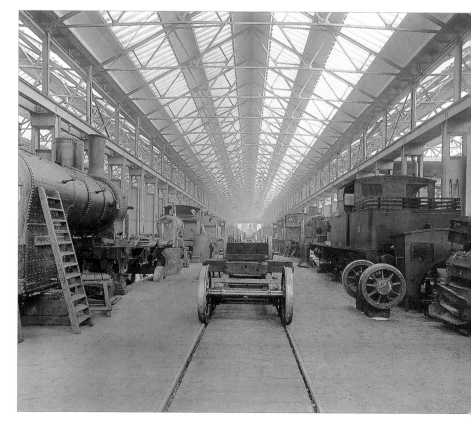

locomotive boilers set up at the back of the shops. It was a feature of living at Eastleigh that, even when walking in the town, one could from time to time hear the ground shake as the large forge hammers did their work. Local people were not only assailed by these noises but also by the works steam hooter which sounded to announce the start and finish of the work time four times a day. Working was usually single shift with an hour's break for lunch (always called the dinner break). Residents also had to cope with the smells from the iron foundry cupola, although this was far worse for people actually working in

the foundry itself of course. However, all this was taken in their stride by Eastleigh's citizens and regarded as a normal part of Edwardian industrial life.

It also has to be said that a large proportion of the inhabitants of the relatively new Eastleigh town in 1909 would have arrived there from London following the transfer of work from Nine Elms, and would no doubt be pleased that such a modern factory was now in full production. Nearly every family living in Eastleigh had one or more members employed within either the locomotive works or carriage works.

Left: **A Drummond 'Paddlebox' Class T14 4-6-0 hangs in the air in the erecting shop. The locomotive is about to be lowered onto its wheels and bogie on the centre track in No 2 or No 3 bay. This photograph shows clearly the ends of the firebox cross-tubes on the 4-6-0. These would be encased by painted covers before the locomotive left the works. In the left background is an Adams Class O2 0-4-4T, while behind it is an earlier Drummond 4-6-0 and a pair of '395' class 0-6-0s is behind that. The practice of using chains to sling locomotives from overhead cranes was eventually regarded as not entirely safe: a chain is only as strong as its weakest link, and one that is about to fail is not often obvious. In the late 1950s, chains were replaced at Eastleigh by wire ropes; at least these begin to unravel if they are about to expire, and that is always detectable in good time!** *Hampshire Museums Service*

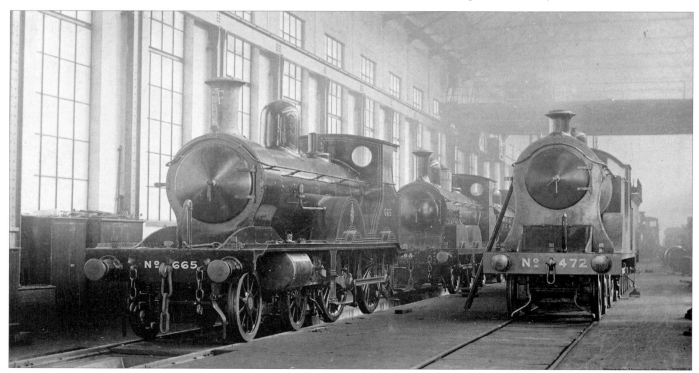

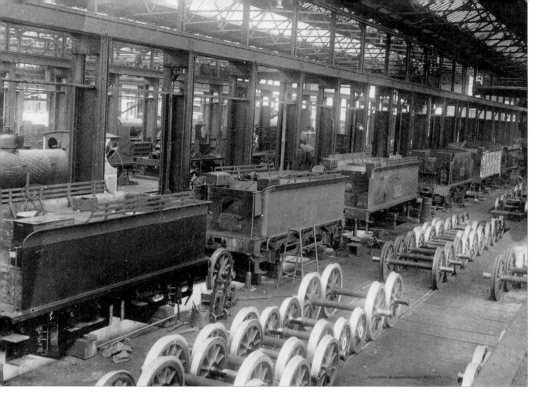

Left: For most of its existence during SR and BR days, No 1 bay of the erecting shop was allocated the work of overhauling and repairing steam locomotive tenders. This early Southern Railway scene shows former LSWR tenders in various stages of repair. Most have still not had their coal rails blocked off with steel plates behind, a modification intended to prevent poor quality coal escaping through them. The tender tank interiors often needed considerable descaling using air-operated hammers, which was a noisy operation. Much of the tender repair work was replacing rusted plate work. *Hampshire Museums Service*

Left: These locomotives are being finished off after overhaul in No 1 bay of the erecting shop. Left, is Adams Class X6 4-4-0 No 665 looking pristine with new paint; behind it is one of the Class A12 0-4-2 'Jubilees', while alongside stands Drummond Class D15 4-4-0 No 472 — his last masterpiece design. *Hampshire Museums Service*

Above: This 1922 picture of the wheel shop shows wheel and journal lathes on the left and a pile of tyres on the right, waiting to be heated in gas rings and shrunk on to their wheel centres. The original wood-plank floor is prominent here. In those days the shop occupied part of what later became the boiler shop. *Hampshire Museums Service*

Above: **At lunch break on 14 April 1960, the wheel shop in No 4 bay is heavily occupied by wheelsets under overhaul. Prominent in this view are Bulleid 'box-pok' wheels with fabricated centres. Wheel and journal lathes are on the left of the shop. The overhead belt drives have long since been removed.** *Colin Boocock*

Left: **High-speed steam locomotives needed their coupled wheels to be properly balanced to minimise hammer-blow to the track. In the 1950s, Eastleigh had a home-made machine, converted from an old wheel lathe, which used springs to identify out-of-balance forces as the wheelset rotated. The weight of lead required in ounces is chalked on the balance weight holding plates.** *Colin Boocock*

Above: **A busy workshop often becomes cluttered and Eastleigh was no exception! The machine shop used overhead belt shafts to transmit the drives to machines. In the middle of this view, *c*1922, is a pair of outside cylinders, still white after painting for marking off to guide final machining. They were almost certainly for a Urie 4-6-0 in view of the inside steam pipe design. The narrow gauge track in the foreground was an idea brought in from Nine Elms Works to move components easily between shops, or to and from the stores. By the 1950s this system had been removed and transport of materials was on the backs of flatbed Lister Auto Trucks. These had single-cylinder petrol engines that sputtered unpleasantly and gave off pungent exhausts, often making the atmosphere inside the shops quite foul. The 1960s saw these replaced by much more eco-friendly Brush battery-electric trucks.** *Hampshire Museums Service*

Right: **By 1960, the machine shop was equipped with rows of lathes, drills, borers, milling machines and shapers. By this time these were usually driven by 'squirrel cage' ac motors. This was just before the era of computer-aided machinery. Some machines could produce a component guided by a template, but the majority relied on a skilled turner or semi-skilled machinist interpreting a drawing correctly and setting the machine to suit.** *Colin Boocock*

Left: The process of marking off plates for cutting by an oxy-acetylene burner and castings and forgings for machining carried on into the 1960s. This 1958 picture shows an apprentice learning how the machine worked when guided by template. *Tony Brown*

Below: The heavy end of the machine shop contained some giant machines. On the right is a big vertical milling machine which is preparing two firebox foundation rings together. Other machines in view are planers and borers. All were driven by the belt system until they eventually received individual electric motors, made more practical when squirrel-cage alternating-current motors became readily available, mostly after World War 2. *Hampshire Museums Service*

Right: There are so many small items on a steam locomotive that are made from brass! Injectors, brakes, pumps, clack valves, manifolds, and all their component parts are brass. The benches in the brass shop at Eastleigh appear in this 1964 view to be swamped by work in progress. Around the corner of the left wall was the brass machining section. *British Railways*

Below: This is the iron foundry in early LSWR days, looking north-west. In the centre are sand moulds in their boxes, waiting for a ladle of molten iron to be swung over them by crane. Workers tipped the ladle gently so that the liquid iron would fill each mould, which was then left to cool. Later, the hardened sand would be broken away and the casting set aside to cool further before being sent for fettling, that is to have moulding flashes and the risers (the channels in which the metal had been poured) cut off. The fettling shop is through the doorways in the right-side wall. A narrow gauge track for distribution of components around the works runs through the shop. *Courtesy National Railway Museum*

Left: This view of the iron foundry in January 1958 shows the same area as the previous photograph, but over 40 years later and looking south. In the foreground are moulds being assembled as well as some that have been filled with molten iron and are cooling. In the left background is the belt circuit of the continuous casting plant with its sand hoppers overhead (set up by the Southern Railway), used for items for which there was high demand. On the extreme right stands a large mould being put together to enable a pair of locomotive inside cylinders to be cast. Emerging through the doorways in the right-side wall can be seen the chutes used to tap the molten iron from the cupola which is out of sight behind the wall. *Tony Brown*

Below: In the iron foundry, final touches are being made to the insides of sand moulds before the hard sand cores are fitted in, around which the molten iron will eventually flow. The foundry was a dirty environment in which to work, the floor being covered with the same black sand as used in the moulds themselves! *Courtesy National Railway Museum*

Right: **Molten iron from the cupola at the side of the iron foundry runs into one of the small ladles, ready to be slung over to fill sand moulds.** *Colin Boocock*

Below: **An advanced feature of the iron foundry that was added by the Southern Railway was a continuous casting belt. Empty mould boxes lie on the moving belt to be collected for refilling in the area in this picture. Here, under the hoppers that deliver sand for making the moulds, workers are preparing some which will subsequently be filled when they get round to the other side of the belt circuit.** *Colin Boocock*

Above: A ladle is tipped to pour molten iron into the risers of the moulds on the continuous belt. The foreground moulds are turning the corner at the end of the belt and will cool as they approach the opposite side, ready for breaking open and emptying. *Colin Boocock*

Below: The biggest castings made at Eastleigh Locomotive Works were those for a pair of locomotive cylinders. This mould is for a Maunsell Class Z 0-8-0T outside and inside cylinder and smokebox saddle combined (the other outside cylinder was a separate casting). Because of its size, the mould sits in a deep pit, but even so, the men have to stand on raised supports. It is critical that the iron is poured in steadily, but with due dispatch, and several large ladles are needed. Should the metal in the mould cool too much before filling is finished, the casting could be porous or otherwise not homogeneous, an expensive error. This one was fine, and was delivered for machining in April 1960. (Eastleigh's iron foundry eventually closed in the early 1960s as part of BR Workshops' rationalisation of manufacturing capacity.) *Colin Boocock*

Right: **The boiler shop abutted the erecting shop bays and stretched across the main building at its south-east end. It occupied two distinct areas, the one in this view being the assembly area for boilers under overhaul. The adjacent section included the marking-off tables and heavy plate cutting and bending equipment. When a boiler had been assembled it was placed outside the shop on a trolley and filled with water; the water pressure was raised to twice the nominal boiler pressure, so that any leaks could be identified and then rectified. Once any repairs had been made, the fire was lit and steam raised to a pressure of 10% above nominal boiler pressure. Only when that test had been declared successful was the boiler ready to be fitted to a locomotive. Eastleigh kept spare boilers for the majority of classes in its care because very often the boiler overhaul took longer than the three weeks of the locomotive overhaul.**
Colin Boocock

Left: **The noisiest part of the works was undoubtedly the boiler shop because of the large volume of riveting and caulking work required to build boilers and keep them water and steam tight. This view shows a Maunsell taper boiler for a 4-6-0 set upside down on a cradle to improve access to the firebox sides. Boilermakers are drilling stay holes prior to threading them and then screwing in the copper stays that hold the inner (copper) and outer (steel) fireboxes together. The drills were powered by compressed air lines, fed from a high-pressure supply that was piped around the works. This pipeline was fed from compressors in the power house at the back of the works site.**
Hampshire Museums Service

Below: **There is plenty of hammering generating lots of noise in the boiler shop in this late 1915 scene. A pair of boilers have had all their firebox stays drilled out and the one on the right is** having a new set of rivets applied around the back of the outer firebox wrapper. The riveter's assistant uses a small coke hearth for heating rivets to red heat. *Courtesy National Railway Museum*

Right: **Making heavy steel forgings required big ovens fired by coke and some hefty steam hammers. Eastleigh's forge was able to form coupling and connecting rods and driving axles. After forging, these big components were taken to the marking-off slab and were then ready to be machined to their final shapes and sizes. Because of the ground vibrations set off by these big hammers, the building was light-framed, and clad with corrugated iron. The sound and vibration from these hammers could be heard and felt in parts of the town!** *Hampshire Museums Service*

Above: **The smith shop used lighter steam hammers to manufacture stressed components such as valve gear parts and brake gear. These were often forged within hardened steel moulds. Like the forge, these hammers were provided with steam from old locomotive boilers placed alongside and outside the shops. In later years these were from old Drummond 4-6-0s. With all these smiths' hearths in operation the atmosphere inside the shop could be choking.** *Courtesy National Railway Museum*

Right: **The brass foundry was a much smaller shop but used basic techniques similar to the iron foundry. In BR years, many of the moulds were made up on machines that could 'bump' the moulds to compact the sand, saving the operative the time and effort needed to do this manually. These machines were operated by compressed air from the works supply.** *Tony Brown*

Left: Components that required considerable hand work, either in assembly or in adjustment, were handled in the fitting shop. This view, looking south-east, takes in the benches for fitting bearings to coupling and connecting rods. These bearings were whitemetalled and machined, and sometimes needed to be scraped to be a good fit on the journals. In the centre stands one of the ubiquitous coke stoves that were the main source of heating in the winter. On a very cold Monday morning after the weekend closure it often took a couple of hours before the shop temperature was in any way comfortable for working. *Tony Brown*

Above: The power house was the source of electricity and other supplies for the whole works. While at Nine Elms steam engines had driven generators to produce electricity for the works, at Eastleigh ac current was brought in from a local power station, and subsequently from the National Grid, and rectified by putting it through rotary converters to produce dc. In later years, more modern three-phase motors needed a 440V alternating current supply, which was obtained through transformers. Most hand tools used in the works were operated either with compressed air, for which compressors were installed in the power house, or a 50V dc supply, for personnel safety.

Outside, adjacent to the boiler shop, there was also a hydraulic tank and ram that provided high-pressure water for the hydraulically driven presses that formed and bent boiler and firebox plates. An overhead crane hoist was present in the power house so that equipment could be removed or replaced when the upgrading of supplies was needed.
Nigel Guppy collection

Right: **The process of rectifying alternating current to produce a semblance of steady-voltage direct current first used rotating machines, an ac motor driving a dc generator. In the 1940s and 1950s new technology enabled ac current to be converted to dc by means of a mercury arc rectifier. This was a vacuum tank containing mercury in which a high-tension ac supply formed an arc that switched between six nodes and a central contact. The output was relatively unrefined dc, but certainly no worse than achieved by a rotating machine, and with lower electrical losses and much less maintenance.** *Tony Brown*

Below: **Seen from across the main line, the front of the works was relatively uncluttered in its early years. On the right stands the main office block in which the management and clerical staff worked. There was also a drawing office and sections for supplies ordering and accountancy. On the extreme left of this view is the single-track gate giving rail access to the front of the works. An Adams 'Jubilee' 0-4-2 stands outside erecting shop No 2 bay while an old 0-6-0ST shunts No 3 bay.** *Courtesy National Railway Museum*

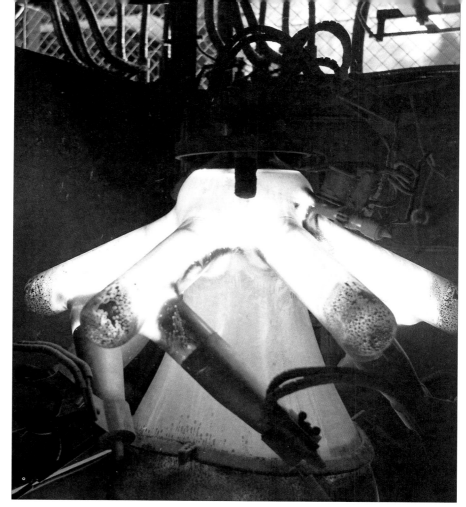

3. Steam locomotive construction

During the period when Eastleigh Locomotive Works was building steam locomotives the LSWR and its successor the Southern Railway had four successive Chief Mechanical Engineers. As mentioned previously, the first two locomotives built there were miniscule 0-4-0Ts of Class S14 for pull-push work, normally with a single carriage. Later products designed under Dugald Drummond's management were at the opposite end of the scale of power. His big, four-cylinder simple 4-6-0s were impressive to look at and, indeed, the Class T14s with their sweeping curves around the smokebox sides and splashers were very handsome locomotives. As so often happens, however, a successful design, such as that of the quality of Drummond's 'T9' 4-4-0, does not always extrapolate well into something very much larger, and so it was with these 4-6-0s. Fortunately, Drummond recognised this in part and was happy to finish his LSWR new building programme with the Class D15 inside-cylinder 4-4-0s. Eastleigh Locomotive Works built 37 Drummond locomotives in total, in the years from 1910 to 1913.

Robert Urie took over as CME in 1912. He had a practical approach to locomotive design that eschewed complication. He liked simple, two-cylinder locomotives with straightforward parallel boilers and outside Walschaerts valve gear and began to build them at Eastleigh in 1914. One key feature of Urie's work was the sheer solidity of his locomotives. Not only were they basic in layout, but their parts had enough metal in them to ensure that none was overstressed.

If the Drummond locomotives had been handsome, indeed beautiful at times, the Urie machines were brutishly powerful-looking. However, Urie had still to learn the need for high-temperature superheat, although to his credit, he did improve on the earlier Drummond steam dryers. Conservativeness in locomotive design was addressed bit by bit and the last of the Urie 4-6-0s, the 'N15s' which became the foundation of the later 'King Arthur' class, were substantially better, being reliable performers well able to haul the heaviest passenger trains of the day, albeit not at breakneck speeds.

The Urie locomotives all had one very good feature in common: they were excellent load haulers and could take heavy, slow-speed slogging in their stride. Thus, his 'S15' class 4-6-0s, including examples of Maunsell's later development, are still performing well today in preservation and have been seen at work in recent years on steeply graded railways such as the North Yorkshire Moors and the Mid-Hants. Altogether, 59 new Urie steam locomotives were built at Eastleigh Works.

When R. E. L. Maunsell came to the Southern as CME

Left: **Most Eastleigh-built locomotives were bigger than those that Nine Elms Works had produced, but an exception was the first two engines built there. These were a pair of tiny Drummond 0-4-0Ts intended for powering one or two-coach push-pull trains. Class S14 No 101, a little larger than the Class C14 2-2-0Ts, was the first new steam locomotive to emerge from Eastleigh Locomotive Works, in September 1910.** *Ian Allan Library*

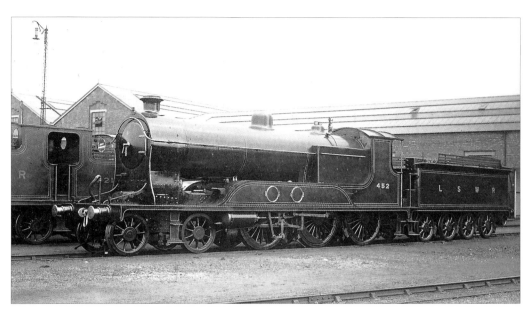

Right: **Drummond produced several small batches of four-cylinder 4-6-0s of which the five Class P14s were built in the winter of 1910-11. No 452 stands outside the paint shop at Eastleigh; the two brass-rimmed inspection covers on the splashers provided access to the outside Walschaerts valve gear.** *Bucknall collection/ Ian Allan Library*

Left: **More successful was Drummond's final class of 4-6-0, the 'T14s' built in 1911 and 1912. These were express engines with 6ft 7in coupled wheels covered by very long continuous splashers. A feature of these was the single, large inspection porthole in the side of each splasher, which gave the class the nickname 'Paddleboxes'. A 'T14' in full flight was an impressive sight and sound and in this view in LSWR days, platelayers stand aside as No 458 thunders past Earlsfield with a West of England express.** *F. Moore's Railway Photographs/Bucknall collection/Ian Allan Library*

at the Grouping in 1923 he brought with him ideas that he had practised at Ashford, these derived from his experiences in Ireland and those of his senior engineers from Derby and Swindon. He believed in high-temperature superheat and higher boiler pressures. Thus, the Maunsell 'H15s' and 'N15s', fitted as they were with longer travel valves of sufficient diameter, were excellent performers. Indeed, the 'King Arthurs', as the 'N15s' soon became known, would be a difficult class to beat when higher performances were needed in the future.

Maunsell's four-cylinder 'Lord Nelson' class 4-6-0s clearly shadowed the Swindon developments; in this class the boiler was parallel but had a Belpaire-shaped firebox with relatively flat top. This enabled a large heating surface to be provided without complicating the staying arrangements. The 'Nelsons' needed further development

to realise their potential and their time would come when Maunsell's successor arrived. In the meantime his team went on to produce the finest and largest 4-4-0s ever built in Britain, the 'Schools' class three-cylinder express engines designed specifically for the Hastings line with its gradients and restrictive loading gauge. The success of this class resulted in further examples built for other routes in the South-East, until 40 locomotives were in stock. Unlike the 'Lord Nelson' class engines, the 'Schools' had round-topped fireboxes. Their performance and economy were legendary and later modifications did little to improve what was already an excellent locomotive design. Altogether, 136 Maunsell-designed engines were built at Eastleigh.

The accession of O. V. S. Bulleid to the position of CME of the Southern Railway in 1937 brought new challenges to the staff at Eastleigh Locomotive Works. His 'mixed traffic' 'Merchant Navy' class 4-6-2s (how else could he convince the Southern Railway board to build large locomotives in war time?) were novel and much more powerful than any steam locomotive type the Southern had owned previously. There were many teething problems, but in time they settled down to perform some prodigious exploits of heavy load haulage and also high-speed, post-war operation. Eventually 30 were built, the last 10 after nationalisation in 1948.

Once Mr Bulleid had modified the 'Lord Nelsons' with Lemaître five-jet exhausts and wide chimneys, and with new cylinders with better steam passages, these engines produced the performances required of them.

Perhaps the stars of the Bulleid era were the light Pacifics: the 'West Country' and 'Battle of Britain' class. Smaller than the 'Merchant Navy' 4-6-2s, these 'light-weights' proved themselves capable of high power outputs and gave performances in some cases barely distinguishable from their bigger siblings. Their wide route availability enabled them to run almost anywhere on the SR. Although 110 were built, only six were completed at Eastleigh, providing the Southern with a powerful locomotive fleet able to cope well with the high demands for post-war travel.

In the middle of the 20th century, Eastleigh Locomotive Works staff exhibited a number of skills levels. Foremost was the staff that included fitters, electri-

Table 1: Locomotives built at Eastleigh Locomotive Works

Class	Wheel arrangement	No built	Years built	Notes
LSWR:				
S14	0-4-0T	2	1910	
P14	4-6-0	5	1910-11	
T14	4-6-0	10	1911-12	
M7	0-4-4T	10	1911	Rest of class built at Nine Elms
D15	4-4-0	10	1912-13	
H15	4-6-0	10	1914	Urie variety
N15	4-6-0	20	1918-19, 1922-23*	Urie variety.
S15	4-6-0	20	1920-21	Urie Variety
G16	4-8-0T	4	1921	
H16	4-6-2T	5	1921-22	
Total LSWR: 93				
SR:				
H15	4-6-0	10	1924	Maunsell variety
N15	4-6-0	10	1925	Maunsell variety
N15	4-6-0	14	1926-27	'Scotch Arthurs'
S15	4-6-0	25	1927-28, 1936	Maunsell variety
LN	4-6-0	16	1926, 1928-1929	'Lord Nelson' class
V	4-4-0	40	1930, 1932-35	'Schools' class
U1	2-6-0	19	1931	Excludes one rebuild (see Table 3)
W	2-6-4T	5	1932	
Q	0-6-0	20	1938-39	
MN	4-6-2	20	1941-42, 1944-45	'Merchant Navy' class
8F	2-8-0	23	1942-44	LMS design for War Department
Total SR: 205**				
BR (SR):				
MN	4-6-2	10	1948	'Merchant Navy' class
WC	4-6-2	6	1949-50	'West Country' class
Total BR (SR): 16				
Total new build: 314				

* Three completed by SR, included in SR total below.

** includes three 'N15s' built by LSWR but not completed until after the 1923 Grouping

Above: **At about the same time as the 'T14s' were entering service, Eastleigh Locomotive Works built the 10 Class D15s which were Drummond's most successful 4-4-0 design. They monopolised the Waterloo–Portsmouth expresses almost until electrification in 1937. No 465 is seen outside the erecting shop at Eastleigh.** *Bucknall collection/Ian Allan Library*

Left: **Urie's impressive-looking if bulky Class H15 4-6-0s were built at Eastleigh. This is new No 483 posing in the works yard. In later years they were modified with Maunsell superheaters and fitted with deep smoke deflectors.** *Ian Allan Library*

cians, boilermakers, riveters, patternmakers, moulders, turners, coppersmiths (pipe-fitters), welders and mill-wrights. These had reached their skilled status by means of five-year apprenticeships backed up by college attendance with City & Guilds examinations. Then there were semi-skilled staff such as machinists, foundry support workers and storesmen. There was also plenty of scope for the employment of unskilled people who took up such duties as labourers and floor sweepers.

Each shop had a chief foreman, while the larger shops

needed assistant foremen also. The men were grouped into gangs led by a working chargehand and among his duties was the collation of piecework records for the gang. Each task undertaken in the works had a piecework price which had been negotiated between the gang and a shop foreman. This value was added as a bonus to a man's basic pay in accordance with the amount of work he had actually produced during the week. In effect it formed the basis of an incentive scheme, and each gang aimed to achieve a given output each week to maintain its earnings.

Left: Class N15 4-6-0s were the principal express engines of the Urie era and were developed by R. E. L. Maunsell. No 747 (later named *Camelot*) arrives at Exeter Queen Street (later Central) station with an express from London Waterloo. Although the locomotive is in LSWR livery, this photograph is likely to have been taken in 1923, the first year of the Southern Railway.
Ian Allan Library

Right: Every locomotive built and indeed rebuilt at Eastleigh Locomotive Works was photographed for the railway records. In the 1920s it was believed that photographic emulsions were not able easily to render the dark green of the Southern Railway adequately, so some locomotives were specially painted in tones of matt grey, including full lining in the railway's style. Urie 'N15' 4-6-0 No 749 was so painted and posed for photography in the works yard when first receiving Southern Railway livery. However, the build date for this locomotive is given as September 1922, which was when the LSWR was still in being, so this photograph is likely to have been taken at the locomotive's first overhaul, or at a special repaint, despite its absolutely pristine condition in which it certainly *looks* new! This locomotive was soon afterwards named *Iseult*, bringing it into the well-known 'King Arthur' class.
Southern Railway/Ian Allan Library

Left: The Urie 'S15' 4-6-0s were 5ft 6in-wheeled versions of the 'H15' and 'N15' classes, specifically designed for fast freight and parcels trains and with an eye on the heavy traffic to and from Southampton Docks. This is No 30512 at Eastleigh depot on 29 April 1959.
Colin Boocock

Top: **The four new eight-coupled Class G16 4-8-0Ts were impressive machines designed by Urie for shunting heavy freight trains over the hump at Feltham yard, west London. This is No 493 seen at Strawberry Hill depot on 24 September 1921, as new and painted in LSWR black livery.** *W. Beckerlegge*

Above: **LSWR light green livery is seen on Mr Urie's new, bulky 4-6-2T No 516 of Class H16. This type was designed to handle heavy, short-distance cross-London transfer freights, which these engines did until dieselisation by BR. Their last duties were to move oil trains between the Esso refinery at Fawley and Southampton Mount Pleasant and Northam yards, and to transfer empty carriage stock between Clapham Junction sidings and Waterloo station.** *Hampshire Museums Service*

Above: One of the initial batch of Maunsell 'King Arthur' class 'N15s' was No 450, seen here in full SR olive green livery and carrying its nameplate *Sir Kay*, as well as brass cabside numberplates. Engines in this batch were reputed to incorporate components from withdrawn Drummond 4-6-0s. No 450 is coupled to a former LSWR eight-wheel 'watercart' tender with inside-bearing wheelsets.

The letter 'E' (for Eastleigh) above *Sir Kay's* number indicates its Western Section origin and was intended to avoid any duplication between numbers of locomotives inherited from the three constituents. Central Section engines had the prefix B (Brighton) and Eastern Section used the letter 'A' (Ashford), all indicating the works responsible for the overhaul of those sections' engines. In 1931 the prefixes were abandoned in favour of adding 1000 to the numbers of the ex-SECR locomotives, and 2000 to those of the former LBSCR fleet. *Ian Allan Library*

Below: The ultimate 'King Arthurs' were the so-called 'Scotch Arthurs', the first 30 of which were supplied by the North British Locomotive Company. The last 14 were built at Eastleigh in 1926 and 1927. 'N15' 4-6-0 No 30793 *Sir Ontzlake* stands at Eastleigh depot after overhaul during British Railways days. The six-wheeled tenders were applied to this batch to enable them to fit on shorter turntables in the South Eastern and Central Sections of the Southern Railway. *Colin Boocock*

Top: There was extreme pride among railwaymen of all persuasions at Eastleigh in the 'Lord Nelson' class four-cylinder 4-6-0s. These handsome express engines were Maunsell's answer to the SR's need for haulage of 500ton express trains at average speeds of 50mph. They did the job, but were not quite as far beyond the performance of the 'N15s' as the operators would have liked. O. V. S. Bulleid, CME of the SR from 1937, modified 14 of the 16 'Lord Nelsons' at Eastleigh with longer travel piston valves, better steam pipes and Lemaître five-jet blastpipes with wide chimneys, which boosted their performance considerably. (All 16 received the Lemâitre system.)

No 850 *Lord Nelson* is seen in its early condition, but after fitting with side smoke deflectors and coupled to a medium-height bogie tender. Later tenders had higher coal bunkers with sloping top raves which added to the locomotives' impressive appearance. *Ian Allan Library*

Above: The 40 Class V 'Schools' three-cylinder 4-4-0s were brilliant locomotives that produced performances out of proportion to their size. Designed for the very restrictive Tonbridge–Hastings route, they were in some ways a truncated 'LN' design but used a shortened and therefore lighter, round-topped Urie-style boiler. These excellent engines were strong yet economical performers and worked heavy Eastern Section expresses until displaced by electrification in 1959 and 1962. This official photograph shows No 919 *Harrow* when new. *Ian Allan Library*

Above: **Most of R. E. L. Maunsell's steam locomotive designs were good-looking and highly competent engines, and the humble Class Q 0-6-0s were no exception, 20 of which were built at Eastleigh for freight traffic. They had steam reversing gear as can be seen in this official photograph of No 534. Mr Bulleid later applied Lemaître exhausts to them, but these proved unnecessary and British Railways fitted the 'Qs' with BR Standard Class 4 blastpipes and chimneys, as carried by the preserved example today, No 541.** *O. J. Morris/Hampshire Museums Service*

Below: **The Maunsell Class U1s were a three-cylinder version of the successful Ashford-built Class U 2-6-0s. Nineteen 'U1s' were built at Eastleigh in 1931, all for service in the South Eastern and Central Sections of the Southern Railway and originally they had a derived valve gear for the middle cylinder. This was replaced later by a third set of Walschaerts gear. No 31907 arrives at Stewart's Lane depot on 31 May 1958.** *Colin Boocock*

Above: The Maunsell 'S15s' had higher-pitched boilers and shorter chimneys than the Urie variety. Both classes found employment on heavy passenger trains during the high summer season, and here No 30830 heads a summer weekend inter-regional train arriving at Bournemouth Central on 4 July 1959. *Colin Boocock*

Below: The 'Lord Nelson' class engines were given Lemâitre five-jet blastpipes and wide chimneys by O. V. S. Bulleid to improve the draughting. No 30863 *Lord Rodney* was stabled at Eastleigh depot on 28 April 1959. *Colin Boocock*

Right: There was a short break in locomotive construction at Eastleigh from 1939 as the war years approached and as Mr Bulleid prepared his first locomotive designs. Most revolutionary were the 'Merchant Navy' class 4-6-2s, all 30 of which were built at Eastleigh, in three separate batches of ten.

The original air-smoothed lines of No 21C1 *Channel Packet*, seen in this official photograph in the works yard, were later compromised by the addition of smokebox top cowling and side smoke deflectors. Their 6ft 2in coupled wheels gave them the necessary 'mixed traffic' status to be built as a contribution to the war effort, and some did indeed work freights for a short season while the engineering of their unorthodox features was refined and made reliable.

The Class MN boiler was without doubt a most prodigious steam generator, and ensured the popularity of the locomotives among footplate crews who knew they could rely on a 'Merchant Navy' to pull whatever loads it was given. Their more unorthodox features were removed during rebuilding by BR from 1956 to 1959, as described in a later chapter. *Ian Allan Library*

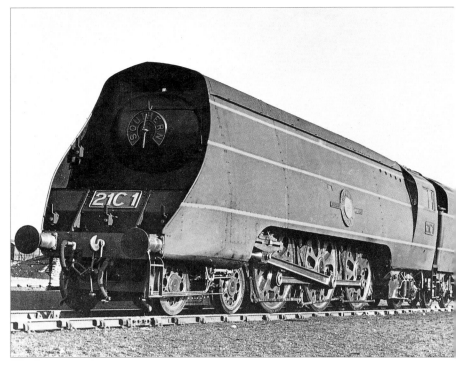

Above: The last engine of the second batch to be built at Eastleigh was No 21C20 *Bibby Line*, seen at Nine Elms depot in 1947. There were differences from the first batch in the treatment of the air-smoothed cabs and front casings, as well as the tender shape. *Colour Rail SR 86/C. B. Herbert*

Left: Locomotive construction at Eastleigh was able to draw on the wide-ranging manufacturing facilities in the works and, for example, new cylinders could be cast in the iron foundry from wood patterns made in the adjacent pattern shop. In this photograph, the shop foreman supervises the insertion of baked sand core pieces into a mould for a locomotive cylinder that is being assembled in the iron foundry.
Hampshire Museums Service

Right: Great care is taken as a cylinder, possibly for a new locomotive, is cast in the iron foundry. Metal has already reached the lower sections of the mould as can be seen from flames emerging from the mould sides. When filling is complete the overflow metal will begin to run down the riser chute in the middle, a hopeful indication that all air has been expelled from the molten metal in the mould.
Hampshire Museums Service

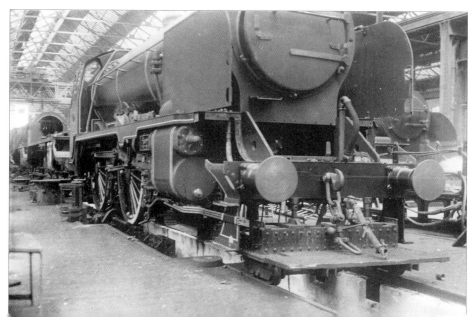

Left: A new 'Schools' class 4-4-0 stands in the erecting shop side pit that contained the valve-setting rollers. In this position, the locomotive's piston valves could be observed in all positions of coupled wheel rotation. Adjustments were made by lengthening or shortening valve gear components, usually the eccentric rod, to ensure that lap, lead and cut-off occurred at the designated points in the cycle.
Hampshire Museums Service

4. The war years, 1939 to 1945

Above: **War work broadened the scope of Eastleigh's skills. In the erecting shop at the locomotive works, 9.2in guns are urgently overhauled and modified for action on the front line.** *Courtesy National Railway Museum*

Referring to Tables 1 and 3 which contain details of construction and rebuilding of locomotives at Eastleigh, one could reach the conclusion that the pace of work carried on with little change during the war years. Nothing could be further from the truth! In reality, some workers were away serving in the armed forces during these difficult years, yet there was an extra need for locomotives to serve the massively increased workload of the Southern Railway during this period. This was met partly by extending maintenance and overhaul intervals, by reducing main line speeds to a limit of 60mph (thus reducing wear and tear), and by working men and machines continuously for very long hours. The need for mechanical overhauls was still there, however, and indeed

was vital to enable the war effort to be served reliably by the railway that was nearest the 'front line', namely the Southern Railway. The SR's role in transporting thousands of troops evacuated from Dunkirk is legendary, as were its efforts to get men and armaments to the south coast in readiness for launching the D-Day landings that so changed the course of the war.

The two main works at Eastleigh were called upon to do much more than railway work during World War 2.

After cessation of hostilities, the Southern Railway published a book explaining the railway's experiences during the 1939-1945 conflict, and fascinating reading it makes, too. There is a short chapter on the railway workshops, mainly concentrating on Ashford, but it is clear that Eastleigh's workload was significantly increased during this period. The locomotive works erecting shop was commissioned early on to overhaul and modify 9.2in howitzer guns. In another project, it manufactured new gun barrels at a reported rate of 60 a month. The brass shop dealt with production of countless details such as fittings for torpedo firing gear, tank components and floats for Spitfire aircraft. The machine shop made parts for Matilda tanks and the boiler shop was engaged in the production of motor landing craft and refuelling barges, final assembly of which was undertaken across the line at the carriage works. There was even production of complex folding tank bridges that a tank could carry and roll out across a void, travel across it and then lift it up again from the opposite side of the gap and carry on its journey. The list of work carried out by the carriage works is just as long. Table 2 lists all types of armaments built in the two works at Eastleigh.

Locomotive construction was not forgotten, and in addition to the aforementioned 'Merchant Navy' Pacifics, 23 LMS Class 8F 2-8-0s were built for the War Department.

Because of the fact that many men were in the forces and yet extra work was being done, the railway workshops took the then unusual step of employing female labour. Figures given are that by 1944 there were 313 women working in the locomotive works and 290 in the carriage works, many of whom also had homes to run and children to bring up in the absence of their menfolk.

It was perhaps fortunate for Eastleigh that the ports of Southampton and Portsmouth were targets of greater priority for the Luftwaffe bombers, or it might have been more seriously damaged. Nonetheless, the efforts of its citizens within the confines of two of Britain's major railway workshops served valiantly to boost the supplies of armaments, this being of enormous benefit to the war effort.

Below: **Construction and fitting out of landing craft was shared between Eastleigh Locomotive Works and Carriage Works. In this photograph an Adams Class O2 0-4-4T pulls away from the carriage works sidings with a trainload of motor launches and landing craft.** *Courtesy National Railway Museum*

Table 2: Armaments work undertaken at Eastleigh Locomotive Works and Carriage Works

Aircraft:
Blenheim conversion sets
Horsa tail plane units
Sabre engine test bed sets
Sabre mounting feet
M.A. tail units
Floats for Spitfires*

Landing craft and boats:
Harbour launches
L.C.S. (M.)
L.C.P. second flight boats
A.L.C.
M.L.C. *
Fuelling tenders
Centre pontoon assemblies
Fast motor boats

Armoured vehicles:
Parts for infantry tanks, Mk IIa *

Scissors bridge layers *
Details for Matilda tanks *

Railway equipment:
23 Class 8F 2-8-0s (LMS type) *
Bogie van conversions (evacuation trains)
Carriages converted for ambulance trains

Guns:
2lb Mk. VII gun mountings
2in U.P. Mk. II pillar boxes
Modification of 9.2in howitzers *
Machining of 2lb Mk X gun barrels *

Miscellaneous:
8,000lb bomb trolleys
Workshop lorry bodies

Bridges and trestles:
30ft self-launching bridges *

* Known to have been carried out in the Locomotive Works.
Main source: *War on the Line — The Southern Railway in Wartime* by Bernard Darwin, published by the Southern Railway Company in 1946.

The work on Spitfire aircraft components at Eastleigh Locomotive Works is commemorated with this photograph of two of these highly successful aircraft flying over southern England. *Ian Allan Library*

5. Steam locomotive overhauls

Above: **By far the most work undertaken at Eastleigh Locomotive Works was the overhaul of the locomotives allocated to it, which were not necessarily just those that had been built there. Indeed, following the cessation of locomotive overhauls at both Brighton and Ashford works in the 1950s and 1960s, Eastleigh became the prime centre for this work on the Southern Region fleet. So frenetic was the erecting shop activity at times that it did tend to become somewhat untidy! On the left in this 1950s photograph of No 3 bay stands 'West Country' 4-6-2 No 34033 *Chard* undergoing intermediate overhaul in which the boiler remains on the frames. Five other Bulleid light Pacifics are behind it, while on the right is 'Scotch Arthur' 4-6-0 No 30781 *Sir Aglovale*. Other 4-6-0s, a couple of 'M7s' and a 'Schools' complete the picture. The wheel shop can be glimpsed to the left in No 4 bay.** *Courtesy National Railway Museum*

The process of overhauling a steam locomotive has additional operations when compared with building new locomotives. Because the locomotive and its components already exist, however, there is obviously much less call on new manufacturing facilities to support an overhaul programme although new components are required if an item is beyond repair.

Locomotives arrived in the works yard at Eastleigh in a short raft, hauled across from the running sheds by the works shunting locomotive. Their arrival was expected and in accord with a programme based on the mileage run by each locomotive, although for most years this translated into a schedule that brought express locomotives in at, for example, two to three-year intervals. General over-

Above: **Looking south-east in the erecting shop, on the left 'King Arthur' 4-6-0 No 30448 *Sir Tristram* has had its driving axle removed for repair. In front is a 'West Country' also undergoing repairs, and beyond that a 'Schools', another 'N15' and a BR Class 4 2-6-4T can be seen. On the right-side pitted track stand three Bulleid Pacifics flanking a Drummond 'T9' 4-4-0; an eclectic mix indeed.** *Dr P. Ransome-Wallis*

hauls at which the boilers were overhauled took place at upwards of five-year intervals, and rarely more than seven or eight years.

When the erecting shop was ready to start on a locomotive it appeared through the end doors on the centre track of the stripping bay. Here, all its components that were scheduled to be removed were disconnected. The smaller items were placed in large steel trays alongside the locomotive while larger items were lifted off and placed on the flat backs of motorised trucks. In the 1950s these were single-cylinder Lister petrol trucks that stank of fumes as they prattled along. These took the components to the shops designated for their overhaul. Happily, the noisy Lister auto trucks were replaced in the 1960s by quiet, Brush battery-electric trucks.

The locomotive was then lifted off its wheels and placed on stands on a pitted side track further into the erecting shop. If necessary, the boiler was removed for overhaul. Reassembly of the locomotive was done in the same sequence as the erection of a new locomotive, as depicted in Chapter 3.

Initially, in SR days, Eastleigh dealt with locomotives from the Western Section, other than those that were of SECR or LBSCR origin which went to Ashford and Brighton works respectively. When Brighton Works closed in the late 1950s Ashford took over most of its work although some locomotives such as the 'N15X' 'Remembrance' class 4-6-0s and 'A1X' 'Terrier' tanks became more common at Eastleigh. When Ashford Locomotive Works closed at the beginning of the 1960s,

Eastleigh took on the responsibility of maintaining all the Southern Region's steam locomotives. As BR's steam fleet reduced further and other works were closed or converted to modern traction overhaul facilities, Eastleigh undertook overhauls of former GWR and LMS types also: Class 5700 0-6-0 pannier tanks and LMS '8F' 2-8-0s for example. Eastleigh was already familiar with LMS designs having taken on the overhauls of the SR's own Fairburn 2-6-4Ts and Ivatt 2-6-2Ts.

Modifications and rebuilds

Major complications to the overhaul process of steam locomotives occurred when they were scheduled to be modified or even completely rebuilt. Depending on the manner or scale of rebuilding, new components of different design would replace older ones, all aimed at improving the performance of the locomotive. At Eastleigh there were several well-known examples of such work.

Mr Urie, for example, had a keen eye for improving the older locomotive stock of the LSWR and he could visualise the potential of some of Drummond's locomotives. Thus he fitted many of them with better superheaters, extending smokeboxes in the process and adorning many locomotives with stovepipe chimneys. After modification, the 66 'T9s' were so good that they lasted well into BR days and earned their deserved nickname 'Greyhounds'. Urie even had a go at improving the four-cylinder 4-6-0s, but it seems that these were basically not right and few survived for long. The exceptions were the 'T14s', which were given new superheaters and were indeed further modified by Urie's successor Maunsell in the early 1930s, this class also surviving into BR days. The Drummond 'E14' and 'F13' 4-6-0s were also stated to have been rebuilt and incorporated into the 'H15' class of mixed traffic 4-6-0s, retaining their numbers from 330 to 335. Little of the original locomotives remained, however, possibly just the frames, wheels and tenders.

R. E. L. Maunsell was able further to enhance the performance of Urie's own machines by judicious upgrading of superheat but, apart from the modifications to the 'T14s', his work was directed more at producing new locomotives.

O. V. S. Bulleid had his own ideas on draughting and modified many of his inherited classes with Lemaître exhausts and wide chimneys in attempts to improve their steaming. The changes to the 'Lord Nelsons' were very effective and removed what had been their main problem: the restricted passage of steam to and from the cylinders.

The Lemaître exhaust system was partially effective on the Urie 'N15s', although not sufficiently so for all 20 locomotives to be modified. All the 'Q' class 0-6-0s were so treated, and were very free running machines, but in their later years these engines ended up with BR Standard single blastpipes and chimneys. Some of the 'Schools' class 4-4-0s received Lemaître exhausts, but the improvement was marginal and not really worth the expense; it is always difficult to improve on the excellent!

In the early 1950s, BR (SR) management recognised that mechanical problems with the Bulleid Pacifics persisted and that their fuel and water economy needed to be improved, as was shown up in the 1948 Locomotive Exchange trials. Eastleigh Locomotive Works had the task of undertaking the rebuilding of these otherwise high-performance locomotives. The work included replacing

Below: **Undergoing its first intermediate overhaul just before Nationalisation, 'West Country' Pacific No 21C105 *Barnstaple* has been reunited with its coupled wheels. Most of its air-smoothed casing has been fitted, but it awaits placing on its bogie and pony truck. On the Southern Railway, and BR Southern Region that followed it, main line locomotives received one or at most two intermediate overhauls between each general overhaul, the frequency of the latter being dictated by the need for a complete boiler overhaul every five to seven years or so. Thus each locomotive was lifted for overhaul in the works after about 50,000 to 65,000 miles of running.** *Ian Allan Library*

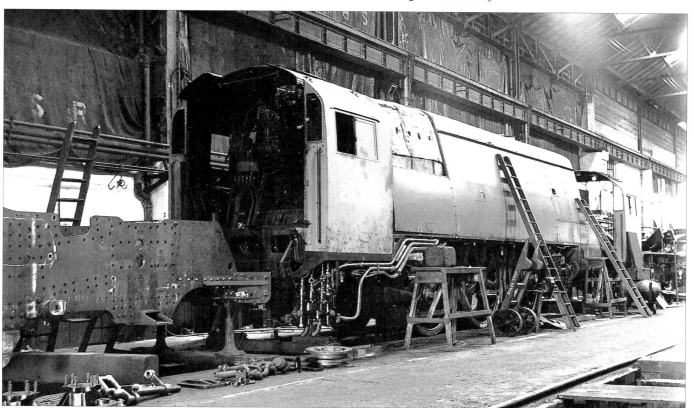

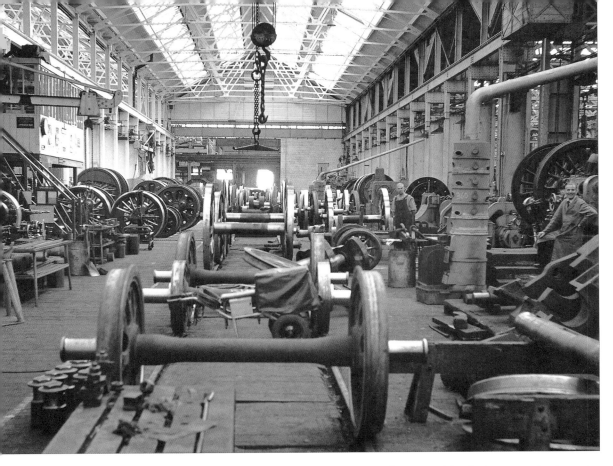

Left: In the wheel shop foreground are tender wheels awaiting attention while overhauled wheels stand beyond, ready for use. The raised wooden building on the left with its unrestricted view of the shop is the foreman's office, similar to those in all the shops in the works. A row of wheel lathes stands on the right side of the shop, and one of the ubiquitous coke stoves is prominent. The variety of wheels is significant.
Tony Brown

the chain-driven Bulleid valve gear with three sets of LMS-style Walschaerts valve gear, casting and fitting new inside cylinders so as to match the alignment of the inside Walschaerts gear and fabricating new extended smokeboxes and new frame stretchers. The air-smoothed casings that gave them their unique and rather grand appearance were replaced by conventional boiler lagging and BR Standard-style side running plates and valances. The rather crude fabricated chimneys and petticoat liners were replaced by properly curved cast liners and chimneys. These and the extended smokeboxes, which surprisingly retained the original oval door, were aimed at improving combustion efficiency. The standard valve gear removed the erratic steam distribution of the Bulleid gear while the elimination of their valve gear oil baths reduced lubricating oil consumption substantially. Fitting manganese steel frame horn liners and axleboxes enabled the intervals between overhauls to be extended from about 65,000 miles to above 90,000 miles.

This was the last major steam locomotive improvement programme completed at Eastleigh Works, and was entirely successful. All 30 'Merchant Navy' class Pacifics, but only 60 of the 110 light Pacifics, had been rebuilt when the programme was halted, the other 50 locomotives remaining in traffic, some to the end of steam on the region. Looking at it entirely in financial terms, the initial cost of £8,500 for rebuilding each locomotive was recovered in fuel economies in a time-span of 6½ years, so BR got its money back on the exercise, just.

In the late 1950s, the BR Board's operating people sent some Ivatt and BR Standard Class 2 2-6-2Ts to the SR to work push-pull trains, oblivious of the fact that the London Midland Region's vacuum push-pull gear was incompatible with the SR's compressed-air system! When these locomotives passed through Eastleigh Locomotive Works for their next overhauls the push-pull equipment was removed and they were fitted with plain, standard steam pipes which improved their appearance at least.

Another activity that added to the interest of working at Eastleigh was the occasional restoration of a steam locomotive for preservation. The works prepared the LBSCR Class A1 'Terrier' 0-6-0T No 82 Boxhill and the LSWR Adams 4-4-0 No 563 for static exhibition at the new transport museum at Clapham. The works did some smartening up of 'Schools' 4-4-0 No 926 Repton and 'M7' class 0-4-4T No 30053 before they were exported to the USA, both of which have since been repatriated to the UK. The full restoration to main line operation of Class S15 4-6-0 No E828 was undertaken within the works by the Eastleigh Railway Preservation Society. This group followed on with the major restoration of the National Collection's 'Lord Nelson' 4-6-0 No 850 Lord Nelson, completed on site in summer 2006, after the official closure of the works.

Table 3: Locomotives rebuilt at Eastleigh Locomotive Works

Class	Wheel arrangement	No built	Years built	Notes
LSWR:				
C14	0-4-0T	2	1913	From 2-2-0Ts
H15	4-6-0	1	1915	From E14 4-6-0
Total LSWR: 3				
SR:				
C14	0-4-0T	2	1922-23	From 2-2-0Ts
H15	4-6-0	5	1924-25	From Class F13 4-6-0s
U	2-6-0	7	1928	From Class K 'River' 2-6-4Ts
U1	2-6-0	1	1931	From Class K1 'River' 2-6-4T
N15X	4-6-0	7	1934-36	From Class L 4-6-4Ts
Total SR: 22				
BR (SR):				
MN *	4-6-2	30	1956-59	'Merchant Navy' class
WCX	4-6-2	60	1958-61	'West Country'/'Battle of Britain' class
Total BR (SR): 90				
Total rebuilt: 115				

* Temporarily listed as 'MNX' until whole class completed

Left:
Following the breakage of the crank axle on a 'Merchant Navy' 4-6-2 at speed at Crewkerne station in 1953, the Southern Region engineers at Brighton quickly developed a process for ultrasonically testing axles to check for flaws and cracks. This soon became a standard procedure for BR as a whole. Here, in the wheel shop at Eastleigh, operator Archie Cross carefully examines the crank axle of No 35029 *Ellerman Lines*. Any flaws would be represented by a sudden blip on the trace on the screen of the oscilloscope. *Tony Brown*

Left: **Even as late in the life of LSWR-built locomotives as 1958 it was possible to see a pair of newly cast inside cylinders (left) being marked off in the machine shop, ready for machining and boring. In the foreground is a Bulleid Pacific inside cylinder probably waiting to be rebored.** *Tony Brown*

Below: **Urie locomotives and Maunsell derivatives had heavy connecting rods with built-up, marine-style big end bearings, as seen in the two foreground rods on this fitting shop bench. Other Maunsell, Bulleid, LMS and BR Standard designs used simpler designs of plain, circular bearings pressed into the rod ends. The bearings were cast in brass, filled with whitemetal for the bearing surfaces, machined and inserted in the rod ends. Where necessary, the bearing surfaces were scraped to present a smooth mating surface to their journals.** *Tony Brown*

Above: **Coupling rods rest on benches in the fitting shop. The machines which stand behind are for boring and grinding bearings.** *Tony Brown*

Right: **After reassembly in the erecting shop, steam locomotives were shunted out into the works yard and moved to the steaming shed outside No 1 bay. On 9 September 1959, 'USA' class 0-6-0 dock tank No 30063, having received its last general overhaul, is raising steam for the trials to take place. After checking for leaks and correcting any found, there would be a brief movement check to see that the valve gear worked correctly. Express locomotives such as Bulleid Pacifics would also be taken out on the Fareham line and run under their own steam to and from the next station, Botley, to ensure the bearings and piston glands were not going to run hot.** *Tony Brown*

Above: **When overhaul and steam trials had been completed, the fire was removed and the locomotive shunted in the late afternoon across to the adjacent running sheds for entry into service and return to its home depot. Ivatt LMS-type 2-6-2T No 41297, having completed its general overhaul and being released on 13 January 1958, was ready to be returned to 72E, Barnstaple Junction shed.** *Tony Brown*

Right: **Not only did Eastleigh Locomotive Works overhaul and repair steam locomotives, it was also capable of fully overhauling the several steam cranes used on the SR for breakdown and civil engineering work. In October 1958, Ransomes & Rapier breakdown crane No DS81 was in the works yard being put through its paces as a final check on the effectiveness of the overhaul work.** *Colin Boocock*

Above: Fresh from a valves and pistons overhaul, in which only the smokebox had been repainted, Maunsell Class N15 4-6-0 No 30783 *Sir Gillemere* takes a heavy freight towards Southampton Docks on 1 August 1957 and passes the entrance to Eastleigh Locomotive Works. This movement was probably the first step in returning the 'King Arthur' to its home depot at Bournemouth. On the left is the Campbell Road ramp to the sharply cornered bridge that forms the very restrictive and sole road access to the works site. *Roy Panting*

Below: Eastleigh Locomotive Works rebuilt many steam locomotives, the rebuild usually being combined with a general overhaul of the mechanical parts and boiler. Robert Urie, for example, had the lone Class E14 Drummond 4-6-0 rebuilt as a member of the 'H15' class. No 335 stands in No 1 bay on 24 April 1920 demonstrating the fitment of its Urie superheater. *Ian Allan Library*

Left: **More prosaic work was the fitting of Robert Urie's 'Eastleigh' superheaters to the more useful locomotives in the LSWR fleet. This included the successful Class T9 'Greyhound' 4-4-0s, such as No 119 seen here in Eastleigh works yard some years after receiving its extended smokebox and losing its Drummond-inspired cross-firebox water tubes. No 119 had just been painted in heavily varnished SR olive green to take up its role as the Southern Railway's royal engine, specifically to work special trains to and from the Ascot races. Very handsome it looked, too.** *Courtesy National Railway Museum*

Right: **By adding superheaters and extended smokeboxes to the Drummond Class D15 locomotives, Urie produced a most successful and powerful express 4-4-0 that worked the Portsmouth 'Direct' line for over two decades before being ousted by electrification. No 470 powers through Earlsfield with the 2.30pm Waterloo to Bournemouth express made up of 13 carriages. The cross-firebox water tubes have also been removed. The supremely clean exhaust was normal on the LSWR.** *Bucknall collection/Ian Allan Library*

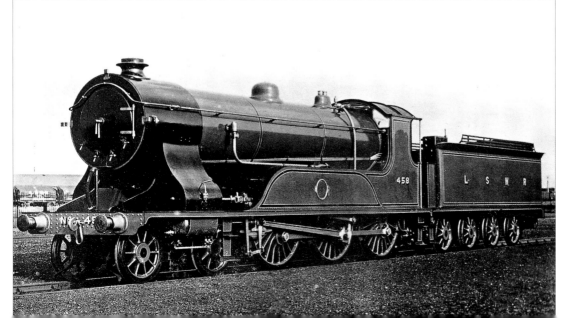

Left: **Urie also modified the more successful Drummond Class T14 'Paddlebox' 4-6-0s with superheaters and extended smokeboxes. Originally built at Eastleigh in 1911, No 458 stands in the works yard in 1915 after completion of this modification.** *Bucknall collection/Ian Allan Library*

Top: A general overhaul included a full boiler overhaul as well as complete repainting of the locomotive. Urie Class S15 4-6-0 No 30510 had just been shunted across to the depot following release from Eastleigh Locomotive Works on 30 April 1959. *Colin Boocock*

Above: Newly rebuilt 'Merchant Navy' 4-6-2 No 35005 *Canadian Pacific*, temporarily classified 'MNX', stands outside the steaming shed at Eastleigh Locomotive Works on 3 June 1959. *Colin Boocock*

Top: In the last year or so of steam locomotive overhauls, the closure of works in other parts of the UK forced BR Workshops to arrange for the overhaul of some former LMS classes at Eastleigh, and occasionally also ex-GWR 0-6-0 pannier tanks so the works staff had to adapt to these unfamiliar types. LM Region Class 8F 2-8-0 No 48408 stands in the works yard in 1965 after a general overhaul. *Colin Boocock*

Above: Another occasional duty at the works was to prepare a locomotive for preservation, either as a static exhibit or as a working example. A static exhibit restored at Eastleigh for export to the USA was 'Schools' class 4-4-0 No 926 *Repton*, seen in the works yard in October 1966 painted in pre-war SR olive green before dispatch to the USA. Fortunately, the locomotive's good mechanical condition enabled its recipients to put it into steam without heavy repair. No 926 later returned to the UK and now works on the North Yorkshire Moors Railway. *Colin Boocock*

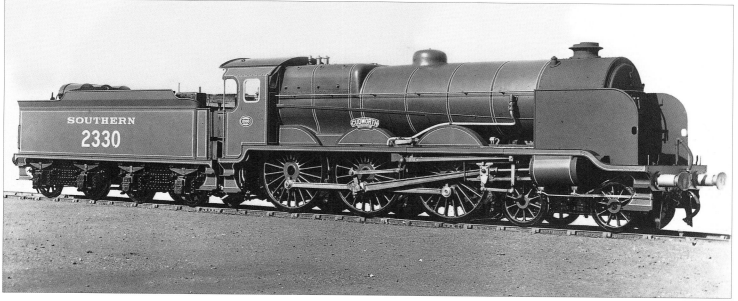

Top: Maunsell modified the 'T14' class further at Eastleigh, increasing the degree of superheat and taking away the characteristic deep splashers to make the external moving parts more accessible for oiling and maintenance. Their appearance still retained a certain grandeur as portrayed by No 460. *Courtesy National Railway Museum*

Above: More interesting rebuilds were carried out in 1934 to 1936 to prepare the former LBSCR Billinton Class L express 4-6-4Ts for life on the Western Section of the SR, following their displacement from the Brighton line by electrification. Mr Maunsell had them rebuilt as 4-6-0 tender engines and as they were considered to be similar in performance to 'King Arthurs' they were given the classification N15X. They received names of notable locomotive engineers of the past, except for No 2333 which was the SR's war memorial locomotive and retained its original name *Remembrance*. In this official photograph taken in the works yard at Eastleigh, No 2330 *Cudworth* shows off its fine lines, in SR olive green livery. *Ian Allan Library*

Left: The biggest rebuilding project undertaken by the works was the transformation of the 30 'Merchant Navy' 4-6-2s and 60 of the 110 light Pacifics into more orthodox locomotives. Under the design direction of Ron Jarvis at Brighton drawing office, the unconventional features of chain-driven valve gear in an oil bath, air-smoothed casing, and steam-operated firehole doors and reversers were replaced by three sets of Walschaerts gear, hand-operated fire-doors and reversers, and traditional boiler cladding and side valances. The octagonal smokebox was replaced by a longer cylindrical one and the fabricated chimney and petticoat by a smoother version in cast iron.

Here, the boiler of 4-6-2 No 35029 *Ellerman Lines* is being lowered on the frames. The white-painted areas of frame show points where magnetic crack detection was undertaken to ensure there were no fractures through corners of rivet holes. This view shows clearly Mr Bulleid's excellent idea in setting the frames slightly closer together so that the axlebox horn guides were supported centrally, not at their outer edges as virtually all other British locomotive types (except the Brighton-designed BR '9F' 2-10-0s). *Courtesy National Railway Museum*

Right: A minor rebuilding was undertaken of five 'USA' class 0-6-0Ts that were being transferred to departmental stock after their displacement from their work of shunting Southampton Docks by Ruston & Hornsby diesel-electrics. The first of these departmental tanks emerged as No DS236 and was one of two destined for Lancing Carriage Works.

The valve gear was rearranged from the original right-hand drive to become left-hand drive to suit the view round the dominant curve at Lancing. The position of the injector controls under the repositioned driver's seat was in fact an advantage because the Lancing locomotives were always single-manned. To match the colour of carriages overhauled at Lancing, the locomotives were painted BR SR carriage green (a darker shade than malachite green) and lined out in black and yellow, Southern Railway style. *Hampshire Museums Service*

Left: By 1960, the erecting shop was being kept in more acceptable tidiness. It is already time for the first few rebuilt 'Merchant Navy' 4-6-2s to receive intermediate overhauls, witness No 35008 *Orient Line* on the left of this view. Air-smoothed Bulleid Pacifics and Maunsell 4-6-0s were also getting intermediate overhauls. At the far end of the shop on 14 April that year stands newly rebuilt 4-6-2 No 34082 *615 Squadron* ready for final assembly after wheeling. *Colin Boocock*

Above: Most years after World War 2, Eastleigh Locomotive Works held an open day for the benefit of the families and friends of employees. Many shops set up interesting displays to show off their work. That in the brass shop always starred nameplates and crests as well as polished-up components such as live steam injectors and connecting rod bearings. This picture of the 1958 brass shop display shows a third nameplate cast for No 34014 *Budleigh Salterton* and two 'Battle of Britain' class RAF badges that might have been appropriate for the last 'BB' 4-6-2, No 34110 *66 Squadron*, but were never fitted to it! *Tony Brown*

Top: The machine shop set up several display tables during open days, including this one illustrating the type of work produced by turret lathes such as those in the background. *Tony Brown*

Above: Shunting the works yard was a busy business at times. One locomotive was always on hand, while a second sometimes appeared when movements to and from the adjacent running sheds were required. The task was usually allocated to Eastleigh depot's oldest goods or shunting engine. In pre-World War 2 days the shunter was often Adams Class 0395 0-6-0 No 0101 (the initial digit indicating the engine was on the SR's 'duplicate list', off the capital stock list). Other '0395s' such as No 30566 were used in early BR days. *Locomotive Publishing Company/Ian Allan Library*

Above: **A surprise to works employees in 1958 was the allocation of the two former Plymouth, Devonport & South Western Junction Railway 0-6-2Ts as Eastleigh Locomotive Works shunters. Nos 30757 *Earl of Mount Edgcumbe* and 30758 *Lord St Levan* started work at Eastleigh when displaced in traffic from their home patch by Ivatt 2-6-2Ts.** *Colin Boocock*

Right: **More depressing work undertaken from time to time at Eastleigh was cutting up unwanted locomotives. Out of the public eye, the first of the Bulleid 'Leader' class 0-6-6-0Ts was dismantled in the erecting shop in 1951. Most locomotives were broken up on sidings in the back of the works yard near the Portsmouth line.** *Stephen Townroe*

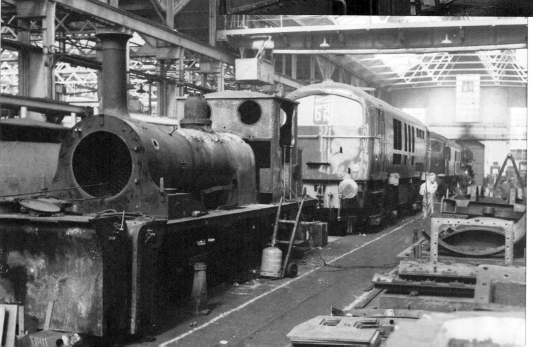

Left: **In No 4 bay, Stroudley Class A1 0-6-0T No 82 *Boxhill* was seen on 14 April 1960 being prepared for exhibition at Clapham Transport Museum. It is in the 'modern' company of Bo-Bo electric locomotive No E5011 and Sulzer Type 2 diesel-electric No D5007.** *Colin Boocock*

Top: **A BBC television news event was arranged to report on the last steam locomotive overhaul (for attention to valves and pistons), at Eastleigh Locomotive Works in October 1966. Rebuilt 'Battle of Britain' 4-6-2 No 34089 *602 Squadron* was specially turned to face the camera and paraded up and down the works yard while works personnel were interviewed.** *Colin Boocock*

Above: **After the end of steam on BR there was still occasional work to be done at Eastleigh. For example, a preserved GWR 2-8-0 came for overhaul late in 1966. No 2818, part of the National Collection, stands in the erecting shop primed and ready for repainting to exhibition standard.** *Colin Boocock*

6. Electric and diesel locomotive overhauls

British Railways Workshops was formed in 1962 to take over the 31 main works from BR's Regions to manage them centrally. A plan was soon produced for the rationalisation of this large number of works, supported by heavy investment for those that were deemed to be required long-term. Eastleigh Locomotive Works was one of these, Ashford was not, and neither were Eastleigh and Lancing carriage works. The Southern Region had already closed Brighton Works in the late 1950s.

The first electric locomotives to appear for regular overhaul at Eastleigh Locomotive Works were the three SR Co-Cos, Nos 20001 to 20003. They immediately caused problems in space allocation in the erecting shop because, unlike a steam locomotive whose components were spread all over the works, the two heavy bogies of an electric locomotive under overhaul occupied an additional erecting shop pit to that taken up by the locomotive body, so erecting shop space became critical for a while.

Supporting the overhaul of these large locomotives was

an enlarged electrical shop. This was set up to undertake complete overhauls of traction motors and of the big motor-generator ('booster') sets that converted the then 660 Volts dc supplied through the conductor rails (raised to 750V in some areas) to the variable voltage dc needed

Below: **Overhauls of the Southern Region's intake of Modernisation Plan diesel and electric locomotives did not become due until the 1960s were well under way. However, the three Bulleid/Raworth Co-Co electric locomotives, Nos 20001 to 20003, had been in traffic for many years. The cessation of this work at Ashford Locomotive Works brought the overhaul of these large locomotives to Eastleigh. On 17 April 1959, for example, No 20001 was awaiting entry into the erecting shop in company with a BR Standard Class 3 2-6-2T. In the background, a Bulleid light Pacific provides steam for the safety valve test house where the blow-off pressures of all overhauled safety valves were set. The steaming shed (far left) is occupied by a BR Standard Class 5 4-6-0 and a Urie Class H16 4-6-2T.**
Colin Boocock

by the six traction motors. This meant that the electrical shop's skills had to be enhanced to undertake full rewinds of armatures and field coils as well as quite complex control apparatus. Later, the shop adopted the modern technique of vacuum impregnation of magnetic coils, ensuring the maximum possible absorption of resin to bond the coils in position and to maintain their insulation.

Doncaster Works started delivering the E5000-type (later Class 71) dc Bo-Bo electric locomotive new to the SR in 1958. Some of these 24 motor-generator locomotives first came to Eastleigh Locomotive Works as part of the commissioning process before they were sent off to work on the Eastern Section of the SR. All returned to Eastleigh Works when their overhauls were required.

From 1957, the carriage works at Eastleigh was delivering the 'Hastings' and 'Hampshire' diesel-electric multiple-units to the SR; the 'Oxted' units were to follow later. All these had English Electric 4SRKT four-cylinder vertical diesel engines with dc generators attached. Overhauls of English Electric engines were soon under way and not just for the DEMUs. The six-cylinder 6KT engines from 350bhp diesel shunters also began to appear at Eastleigh for overhaul, as did the 4SRKT units also used in the E6001-series (later TOPS Class 73) electro-diesel locomotives. (The first six of these electro-diesels, incidentally, were the only locomotives ever built in Eastleigh Carriage Works.)

A new diesel shop was established in part of the erecting shop and this was a period of considerable change within the works. Under works manager R. A. Bolton the works heating stoves were replaced (not before time) by oil-fired air heaters with thermostatic control. A new production and planning office was set up in a wooden-framed building outside the erecting shop; its role was to ease the burden of the shop foremen in interpreting the rapidly increasing number of new instructions and designs being dealt with by the works. This was later expanded when initial and finished work inspectors were added to the works production system under BR Workshops' national policy.

The Southern Region of BR began to need repair and overhaul attention to its newly acquired fleet of 98 Type 3 BRCW/Sulzer diesel-electric Bo-Bos, later to be known as Class 33s and affectionately as 'Cromptons', an acknowledgement of the ruggedness of their Crompton Parkinson electric traction equipment. These were allocated to Eastleigh Locomotive Works for overhaul which necessitated the enlargement of the diesel engine shop. This was extended to occupy part of No 1 bay that had once been the tender shop alongside the Portsmouth line. The eight-cylinder Sulzer 8LDA28 engines gave the works plenty of headaches with problems such as crankshaft fractures and cylinder liner leakage, but the works soon found ways of meeting these challenges.

After overhaul the Type 3s were shunted to the new test house at the back of the works. This was equipped

Left: **By 1966, the works was well into the transition from steam to modern traction overhauls and repairs. This view of the erecting shop shows BR Standard Class 4 2-6-0 No 76005 and 'West Country' 4-6-2 No 34023** *Blackmore Vale* **(since preserved) and another BR Standard keeping company with two BRCW Type 3 Bo-Bo diesel-electrics and one of the early Co-Co electrics.** *BR Workshops*

with rows of static resistors that acted as load banks for the power units of locomotives being set up, tested and run in.

During this period the traditional, jealously guarded territory of each grade of skilled staff began to be eroded. It was sensible to multi-skill some people so that they could undertake related tasks on the new forms of traction. Thus fitters and electricians in particular began to be trained to undertake jobs formerly done only by the other grade, an entirely logical step when considering that much

Left: **Type 3 Bo-Bo No D6553 nears completion of its overhaul in 1966. The chart on the lower bodyside is a progress diagram based on the network analysis schedule which enabled the erecting shop work on one of these locomotives to be completed in 13 shifts, or 6$\frac{1}{2}$ working days. The success of this schedule relied on concentrated attention by up to 12 men working in, under, outside and on top of the body, all at the same time!** *BR Workshops*

Right: **The network analysis-based overhaul programme was successful and continued in use for many years. No 33001 is seen under overhaul at Eastleigh on 3 May 1976, and displays the progress chart on its cab front.** *Brian Morrison*

Above: **There was considerable variety of work in the erecting shop even in 'modern traction' years! In No 3 bay, two Class 33 diesels, Nos 33119 and 33204, receive intermediate overhauls (then scheduled for every three years) while Ruston & Hornsby Class 07 0-6-0 diesel-electric No 07006 from Southampton Docks is under repair. Work is also under way on Class 71 Bo-Bo dc electric locomotive No 71003 (formerly No E5003).**
Brian Morrison

electrical engineering employs mechanical engineering principles, and that the assembly of much electric traction equipment demands mainly mechanical skills.

The search for greater effectiveness always goes on. In the later 1960s the planning technique known variously as critical path analysis or network analysis became available, having just been trialled successfully at Doncaster Locomotive Works. Eastleigh was one of the works that took it aboard quickly. The technique required vector diagrams to be drawn that depicted each activity in the overhaul process, and showed how all the activities inter-related, together with how long they were each expected to take. By assessing the longest path through a diagram (called the 'critical path') the works was able to determine the minimum time a locomotive overhaul could take. In the case of the Type 3s, an intermediate overhaul plus the first-time fitting of AWS equipment used to take about

three weeks of double-shifted erecting shop time. When the schedule had been amended in the light of network analysis, this time was reduced to about seven working days and nights (13 shifts). The technique was extended to the overhauls of Southern Region electric and electro-diesel locomotives.

In 1965, there had been an experimental modification of Sulzer Bo-Bo diesel-electric No D6580 for push-pull operation. This had been used for about a year working with a de-motored EMU on the Clapham Junction to Kensington Olympia service.

The Class 74s were conversions of 10 E5001-series electric locomotives done at Crewe Works. They retained their motor-generator 'booster' sets as well as receiving Paxman diesel power units; thus they were dubbed 'boozels' by irreverent lay people.

This was followed by the conversion at Eastleigh of a further 19 Sulzer Type 3 Bo-Bos for push-pull working, including modifying No D6580 to conform to the final design. These later became Class 33/1. This work was completed on time, which was just as well because the parallel work on producing the Class 74 electro-diesels at Crewe ran late (as did delivery of the new 4-REP EMU power cars) and so the '33/1s' were crucial in powering some of the services on the Bournemouth line from July 1967 even though this was newly electrified.

Above: **One of the Class 71 Bo-Bo electric locomotives is lifted off its bogies in No 2 bay, ready to be placed on a side pit elsewhere in the erecting shop. Class 33 No D6545 is already resting on stands on the adjacent side pit. The blank wall indicates the position of the electrical shop in No 1 bay where traction generators and motors were overhauled.** *BREL*

Below: **The English Electric 4SRKT diesel generator power units from the 'Hastings' and 'Hampshire' DEMUs were already needing overhaul by 1960 and a shop had been established for this at the south-east end of No 2 bay. This view shows an overhauled engine and generator being reassembled. The shop also took on the overhaul of EE 6KT power units from 0-6-0 diesel-electric shunting locomotives of Classes 08 and 09.** *Colin Boocock*

Left: A new electrical shop was set up in No 1 bay, capable of dismantling and fully overhauling the dc traction motors and generators of the new types of locomotives. *BREL*

Right: This armature has been overhauled and is having its steel centrifugal bands soldered into position. These are to prevent any mechanical lifting of the armature coils in their slots when rotating at high speed. This armature's commutator copper segments were in good condition; the works had decided on this occasion not to skim the commutator in a lathe, relying on the wear rate continuing to be low, due to its existing work-hardened surface. *Tony Brown*

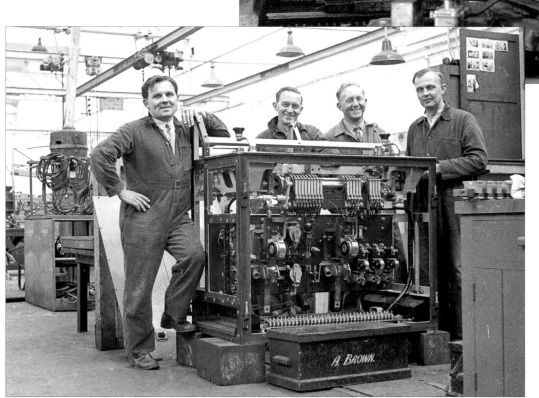

Left: It was not just big motors and generators that underwent overhaul in the electrical shop; locomotive controllers and associated relays and valves provided a challenging overhaul task. In September 1960, this group of electricians were pleased to show off their handiwork following completion of the overhaul of a control cabinet for an EE 350bhp diesel-electric shunting locomotive. *Tony Brown*

Above: **Another type of locomotive that came to Eastleigh Locomotive Works for occasional overhauls and repairs was Class 74.** These 10 locomotives had been rebuilt from Class 71 electric locomotives to become electro-diesels by being fitted with Paxman diesel-generator sets. They retained their original motor-generator sets for electric working off the conductor rail but could work away from conductor rail areas by switching from third rail pick-up to diesel operation, and so were able to work boat trains and freights into Southampton Docks. No E6104 hums through the new Southampton Airport station, south of Eastleigh, in 1969. *Colin Boocock*

Below: **The 1962 Workshops Plan promoted considerable investment in the layout of Eastleigh Locomotive Works to cater for the new forms of traction (as described in Chapter 7).**

A new diesel power unit test house was built near the back of the works yard to enable the loading and setting-up of the more powerful Sulzer 8LDA28 engines and generators in the BRCW/Sulzer Type 3 Bo-Bo diesel-electric locomotives.

All 98 of these locomotives had been supplied to the Southern Region to assist in the elimination of steam traction. The test house was flanked by two rows of static resistances with remotely operated switches to provide the load for the generators during load testing. One of these resistance houses can be seen in this view to the right of the main test house building. These neat Type 3 locomotives, later known as Class 33s and nicknamed 'Cromptons', were BR's first diesels to be dual-braked and capable of supplying electric train heating. *Colin Boocock*

Above: **Outshopped from Eastleigh in the new BR Rail blue livery in 1966, Class 09 0-6-0 diesel-electric shunting locomotive No D4100 looks very smart indeed.** *Colin Boocock*

Right: **A small test facility, seemingly of a temporary nature, was provided for electric locomotives that had been overhauled. It was sufficient to place a locomotive on a track with a third rail and to make sure that the controls and motor-generator sets were both actuated and that motor rotation was correct. No 20001 stands in the facility in February 1967, this being the only one of the three dc Co-Cos to receive the new BR Rail blue livery. It was the last locomotive on the Southern Region to carry a steam-heating boiler for the supply of train heat, normally used only for the royal train. By summer 1967, all SR passenger stock was fully air-braked and electrically heated.** *Colin Boocock*

Right: **To move English Electric 4SRKT diesel power units between the depots at St Leonard's, near Hastings, Eastleigh and the Locomotive Works, a small fleet of four-wheeled wagons was established in departmental stock. These had floor mountings similar to those in the DEMU engine rooms to which the power units were secured for transit. The loads were protected by lightweight canopies, as seen on this last surviving wagon, photographed at Eastleigh in July 2005.** *Colin Boocock*

Below: **Training of apprentices was encouraged by the setting up of a new training school. This had a useful workshop facility in which young people were taught their skills under helpful supervision. The attached classrooms were available also for other training. The school was so successful that other companies in the area sent their trainees there.** *BREL*

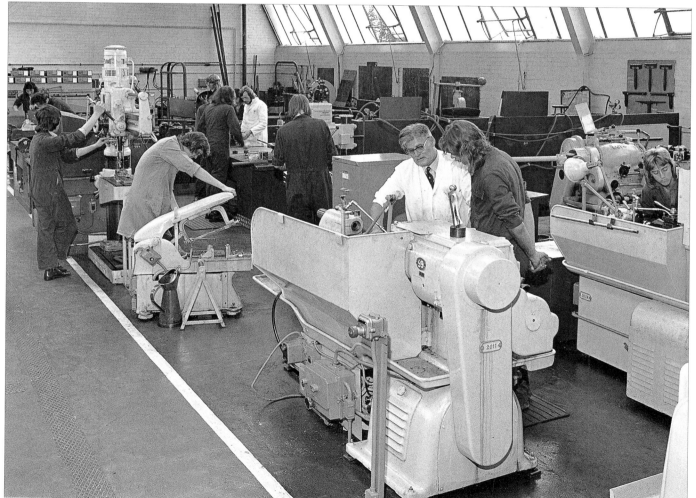

7. Absorbing the carriage works

The 1962 Workshops Plan substantially affects the history of Eastleigh Works because of the decision to transfer the carriage overhaul activity from the separate carriage works into the locomotive works, despite the fact that the carriage activity occupied a greater area of factory buildings. The Workshops Plan envisaged the transfer taking place in 1967, after steam locomotive overhauls and repairs had ceased altogether at Eastleigh, the Southern Region abandoning steam working on all its lines in July. Scheduled steam locomotive overhauls at Eastleigh Locomotive Works were therefore not needed beyond late 1966.

The new carriage overhaul layout was a classic example of progressive working. It occupied the space formerly taken up by erecting shop No 4 bay, the wheel shop and the fitting, machine and boiler shops (the latter in part). The idea was that carriages of all types to be overhauled would enter No 4 bay from the south-east end and pass through 11 stages (Nos 1 to 11) to emerge in the front works yard. Those that required heavy C1 and C2 body overhauls (see the table at the end of this chapter for a description of these BR overhaul classifications), would then be moved by a new traverser into the second half of the layout and pass through another 11 stages (Nos 12 to

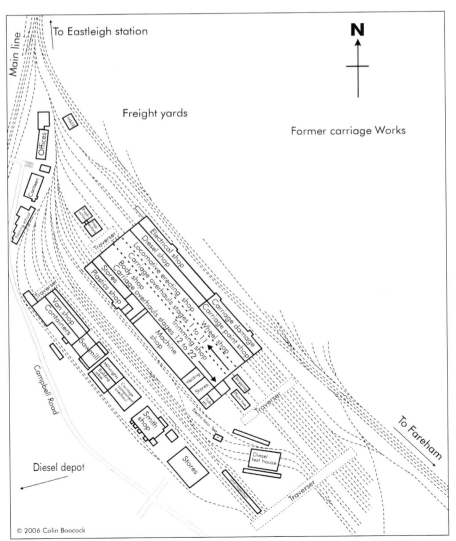

Left: **Figure 4: Eastleigh Works post 1967.**

Top right: **The original carriage works at Eastleigh was a large factory divided between several buildings connected by railway tracks and with traversers to facilitate movements between adjacent workshop tracks. New Bulleid-style, steel-bodied electric multiple-unit carriages, constructed on underframes from old timber-bodied EMUs, were assembled in Eastleigh Carriage Works in the post-war years. The vehicles were built using a 'progressive belt' system in which they were moved up to different stages as the work progressed.** *Hampshire Museums Service*

Right: **The closure of Lancing Carriage Works in the early 1960s caused BR Workshops to concentrate Southern Region carriage overhauls on Eastleigh Carriage Works. In this February 1967 view, a 2-BIL EMU motor coach is in the lift shop of the old works ready to be lifted on to stands while its bogies are overhauled. The steam comes from the bogie cleaning facility known as the 'bosh'.** *Colin Boocock*

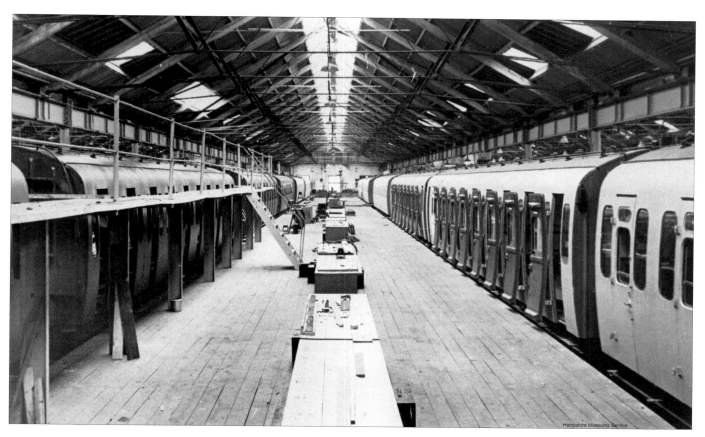

22) to emerge at the back of the works again, ready to be moved on a traverser in the back of the works yard, across to the paint shop. This had been set up in the east end of the former boiler shop and extended into No 2 bay of the old erecting shop. Lighter overhauls of the C3 and C4 type were drawn off the first half of the layout after Stage 11 when complete, C3s being moved for painting and C4s being already complete and ready for dispatch.

It was seen as a bold move to squeeze the layout down to 22 stages overall (excluding those in the paint shop) because the carriage works at that time had been undertaking this work in over 40 stages. The intention was to maintain the same rate of output, so a big reduction in carriage downtime was anticipated. Many people in the works believed that this scheme would not work as they were convinced that the layout did not allow enough space and time for all the activities. Something like 23 to 26 lifts a week were required to be done in stages 1 to 11 to achieve the overhaul programme, of which around 11 or 12 would be C1s or C2s needing to pass through Stages 12 to 22 also.

Fortunately, the network analysis technique was being trialled at that time, as mentioned in Chapter 6. This showed the length of the critical path for a C1 overhaul to be safely inside the time a carriage would need to pass through the layout. By adding resources to the diagram, the project team demonstrated how and where each activity could take place on the new layout. This led to a revised and highly practical plan of working that, when explained to staff representatives in a number of conference sessions, was convincing in its simplicity.

Between the two tracks was a wide space in which much of the carriage component repair or overhaul work would be done. This included a large area for retrimming seats and seat backs with new moquette. Other areas were set up nearby for overhauling slam doors and other components.

The sequence followed by a carriage was for it to enter the shop at the back of the works and visit Stages 1 and 2, where stripping took place during which most components were removed. At Stage 3 the carriage body was lifted off its bogies and swung sideways to sit on high, wheeled stands ready for progression along and between the high work platforms. The bogies were overhauled in the same bay alongside the carriages. A new system was introduced whereby a list of bogie components needed for a standard overhaul plus common extras was sent to the stores in advance of the carriage appearing in the shop. The stores placed all these parts on metal stillages (known always as 'Christmas trees'). The stillage was conveyed by truck to a position alongside the bogies being overhauled, and the new parts were used to overhaul the bogies. The parts removed from the bogies took their places on the stillages, which then moved back to the stores where arrangements were made for the components to be repaired and overhauled ready for reuse when required for another bogie. This effort made it possible to keep the progressive layout moving because any potential shortages of parts would be revealed in good time to be resolved.

In Stages 4 to 9 the carriage underframe received all its overhaul needs including removal and replacement of such items as belts and generators, batteries, brake cylinders, pull rods and levers. Overhead, men and women working on the high platforms undertook the overhaul process for the carriage body including on C3s the preparation of the body surface for painting. Stage 10 brought the body and bogies back together again and all connections were completed before the carriage was pulled out from Stage 11 into the open air.

The opposite side of the layout saw heavy body overhauls continued as doors and seats were refitted, door welts replaced and the newly overhauled door locks checked, lined up and tested. Interior work included the overhaul of lighting as required, cleaning of facings and revarnishing of woodwork. A major job, done on all C1 and C2 overhauls, was replacement of floor linoleum. By the time the carriage reached Stage 22 it was ready for movement to the paint shop. Figure 5 outlines what happened at each stage.

If a DEMU, such as a 'Hastings' power car, needed its power unit overhauling, this was lifted out at Stage 3 by the same overhead cranes that then lifted the vehicle itself off its bogies. A replacement power unit would be fitted at Stage 10.

Below: **In the trimming shop in the old carriage works, seat cushions and backs are stripped, refilled and covered in new moquette. Surrounding the working area is a continuous belt on which hangs work waiting to be done and also the finished items ready to be stacked near the vehicle positions.**
Colin Boocock

The paint shop was also laid out on a progressive basis. This was an eight-stage layout with a traverser at the blunt end of the shop to take the carriages across from one road to the next. The former carriage works had already adopted the spray painting technique that was in vogue in the 1960s and 1970s, using uroalkyd 'one-coat' paint. The BR blue-and-grey livery had its on-costs in extra time spent sticking on the white plastic lining bands and the additional masking to keep one colour from the other when the spray guns were in use.

The transfer from the carriage works of carriages and most of the workers was undertaken over a three-week period. One of the authors was Repairs Engineer at the time and had arranged with the Southern Region shopping control to regulate the classifications of carriages coming into the layout so that lighter overhauls came first. Thus the stages 1 to 11 part of the layout was set up and working with C3 and C4 overhauls before life got more complicated when C1s (which were still then running through the old carriage works) began to be fed into the layout. To ensure the right vehicles arrived in the right order and that the mix of workload was containable, a very small control centre was established on the works. This centre issued a list of vehicles needed in the shop ready for each morning, the role of the yard foreman being critical in ensuring this all went to plan.

The works did not want to have lines of carriages standing waiting overhaul. Therefore, arrangements were

Above: **Some considerable investment was needed to accommodate the carriage overhaul layout in the Locomotive Works main building. This view looks along the boiler shop area during the transition period in 1966 and shows a wall being built between the truncated boiler shop and what was to become the carriage paint shop. An EMU motor bogie frame is undergoing attention in the foreground.** *Colin Boocock*

made with the SR to drive electric multiple-units (the bulk of the workload) from Wimbledon depot direct to the works yard so as to arrive the day before the first vehicle of that unit was to be fed into the progressive layout. The SR co-operated brilliantly, and downtime was reduced to the minimum ever achieved in a BR works. For example, a C4 overhaul for a four-car EMU averaged no more than four days, a C3 no more than seven and C1 overhauls were going back to Wimbledon for commissioning about a fortnight after being sent to Eastleigh. In 1966, there were over 300 carriages on the old carriage works site at any one time. By early 1968 the combined works had reduced this to just 110 including numerous parcels vans!

BR Workshops' monthly costings of carriage overhauls listed each works' achievements so that they could be compared. The only carriages that Eastleigh overhauled that were common with other works were C3s and C4s to Mk 1 locomotive-hauled stock. Before the author left Eastleigh he was gratified to see that Eastleigh's cost of C3 output was lower than at any other works, this despite persistent criticism by Derby headquarters that Eastleigh's old-fashioned piecework system was too expensive! (In fact, the high bonus payments made to staff in the system appear to have been largely because productivity at Eastleigh was so high.) The success of this new carriage overhaul layout owed so much to the inspired leadership of the works manager of the combined works, Lancelot Sanders.

When the iron foundry had closed back in 1962 the space was developed for a new activity for the locomotive works: the repair and overhaul of containers. These were not the modern ISO containers but the smaller maroon-painted boxes carried by BR on short-wheelbased flat wagons. This activity had declined by 1967 and so a part of the shop was developed under the Workshops Plan to overhaul four-wheeled vans such as PMVs and CCTs on a small progressive layout. Supporting this was a sawmill alongside, so the atmosphere in the shop had changed over the years from the suffocating smells of the former iron foundry to the more pleasant aroma of newly cut or planed timber. The painting of these vehicles was undertaken in situ, rather than using up valuable space in the carriage paint shop.

The transfer of so many people from the carriage works brought the total staff at Eastleigh Works to 2,500. These included many skills hitherto not known on the site. Carriage-specific skills included bodymakers, finishers, plumbers (who repaired slam door locks), paviors (who laid floors in vans) and carpenters, although the latter grade had been present in the locomotive works as part of the works maintenance teams.

Carriage overhaul codes (BR late 1960s)

C1 Lift vehicle, overhaul bogies, underframe equipment, traction equipment, overhaul vehicle interior complete, revarnish interior wood panels, replace floor linoleum, replace seat trimming, replace corroded body members and cladding, repaint vehicle.

C2 Lift vehicle, overhaul bogies, underframe equipment, traction equipment, overhaul vehicle interior complete, revarnish interior wood panels, replace floor linoleum, replace corroded body members and cladding, repaint vehicle.

C3 Lift vehicle, overhaul bogies, underframe equipment, traction equipment, light interior attention, revarnish interior wood panels, repaint vehicle.

C4 Lift vehicle, overhaul bogies, underframe equipment, traction equipment.

C5 Unscheduled repair.

C6 Light interior attention, revarnish interior wood panels, repaint vehicle.

Right: **The Locomotive Works machine shop was photographed in 1966 just before it was moved to the former smith shop space.** *Colin Boocock*

Left: **The machine shop was fully established in its new site by early 1967. The old coke stoves had been replaced by effective oil-fired air warmers, one of which is prominent by the far end wall.** *Colin Boocock*

Left: Just after erecting shop No 3 bay had been partially vacated in late 1966, work was under way in demolishing and filling in the pits in preparation for laying a new concrete floor for the repositioned wheel shop. A deep pit is under construction by contractors to accommodate a wheel lathe. In a reduced area in the background, erecting shop work continues on electric locomotive No 20003 and three steam locomotives. *Colin Boocock*

Below: At the same time in 1966, No 1 bay of the former erecting shop has been stripped out and new flooring laid for the electrical shop which will overhaul the much greater volume of traction motors and electric control gear arising from multiple-unit carriage overhauls due to start the following year. A solitary London Midland Region Class 8F 2-8-0 stands looking in bemusedly. *Colin Boocock*

Right:
By early 1967 the machine shop had been relocated, the boiler shop closed down, No 4 bay of the erecting shop had been stripped out and the whole combined area made ready for construction of the new staging for the carriage overhaul layout. This view shows (left background) the former fitting shop area and, right, the high staging that would surround carriages progressing through Stages 4 to 9 of the new layout. A Class 33 and three diesel shunting locomotives temporarily occupy what will be the area around carriage overhaul Stages 10 and 11, while No 2 bay of the erecting shop is being refurbished for future locomotive overhauls. *Colin Boocock*

Above: The iron foundry had closed in 1962 and the building had been used for repair and overhaul of containers. BR once owned a large fleet of small containers, mainly of type BD, which fitted on the back of a 20ton lorry and needed nothing bigger than a 10ft wheelbase, four-wheeled Conflat wagon for transport around the railway system. Their use was declining by 1966, however, due to the rapid expansion of the use around the world of the much bigger ISO containers. The container shop was moved so that half the former iron foundry area could be adapted for overhauls to four-wheeled vans such as CCTs and PMVs. The pattern shop and brass foundry areas became the associated sawmill. *BREL*

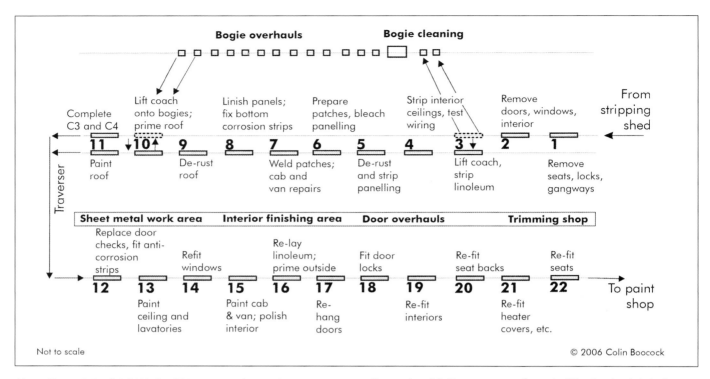

Bogie overhauls   Bogie cleaning

From stripping shed

Traverser

Complete C3 and C4	Lift coach onto bogies; prime roof		Linish panels; fix bottom corrosion strips	Prepare patches, bleach panelling		Strip interior ceilings, test wiring	Remove doors, windows, interior

11 | **10** | **9** | **8** | **7** | **6** | **5** | **4** | **3** | **2** | **1**

Paint roof | | De-rust roof | | Weld patches; cab and van repairs | | De-rust and strip panelling | | Lift coach, strip linoleum | | Remove seats, locks, gangways

Sheet metal work area   Interior finishing area   Door overhauls   Trimming shop

Replace door checks, fit anti-corrosion strips		Refit windows		Re-lay linoleum; prime outside		Fit door locks		Re-fit seat backs		Re-fit seats

12 | **13** | **14** | **15** | **16** | **17** | **18** | **19** | **20** | **21** | **22**

To paint shop

Paint ceiling and lavatories | | Paint cab & van; polish interior | | Re-hang doors | | Re-fit interiors | | Re-fit heater covers, etc.

Not to scale

© 2006 Colin Boocock

Above: **Figure 5: Eastleigh Works, 1967: Progressive carriage overhaul layout.**

Below: The new layout quickly established itself in 1967 as a fast and reliable method for progressing carriage overhauls. In Stage 3, a 'Hastings' DEMU coach is being lifted ready to be swung across so that it can enter the high staging. Two vehicles from a Portsmouth 4-COR express EMU are already being worked on in Stages 4 and 5. One power car from the 'Hastings' unit is in Stage 6, extreme right. Bogie overhauls are in hand on the parallel track (left) having passed through the cleaning bosh which is the square structure behind them. On the right, in front of the high staging, are the bogie component stillages ('Christmas trees') each of which carried enough spares to enable one bogie to be fully overhauled. Used components were returned to the main stores on the stillages to simplify materials handling. *Colin Boocock*

Right: **The trimming shop was set up on the main carriage overhaul staging so that workers could retrim seats and seat backs close to where they would be refitted to the carriages. This picture shows clearly the conveyor system that brought unfinished and finished products around to their respective work stations.** *BR Workshops*

Below: **When BR threatened to replace the 'Brighton Belle' Pullman EMUs with more modern 4-CIG and 4-BIG electric units there was uproar among the great and the good Brighton line commuters! BR therefore decided to overhaul the three five-car Pullman trains just once more in 1968. They were repainted into BR blue-and-grey livery with an** *ersatz* **old-fashioned lining style formed of white plastic lining tape and the 'Brighton Belle' train name applied in white paint on the carriage sides. You either liked it, or you didn't.**

The appalling ride of these old units on their single-bolster bogies with undamped suspensions compared unfavourably with the good ride of the B5-bogied CIGs and BIGs, providing a good reason to withdraw the Pullmans finally in 1972. This photograph shows the train on its last day of operation, Sunday, 30 April 1972, passing through the South Downs at Patcham. *G. R. Mortimer*

Above: **When BR Mk 1 express EMUs were overhauled in the new layout at Eastleigh Works they were repainted in blue-and-grey livery with dark brown underframes and bogies; the latter later changed to traditional black. This 4-BIG unit, No 7035, for Brighton main line services stands in the works yard ready for dispatch under its own power direct to Wimbledon depot. This is where overhauled units were recommissioned for speedy re-entry into revenue-earning service after overhaul.** *Colin Boocock*

Below: A train of GUV parcels vans was overhauled at Eastleigh in 1967. Repainting was by spray uroalkyd gloss paint that afforded good cover and was of a thickness which was supposedly resistant to wear from carriage washing plants. The decals including the double-arrow symbol were stuck to the bodysides as pre-masked plastic 'transfers'. After paint spraying, the masking layer was removed, revealing the shiny white lettering. One idea behind this was that the transfer did not project above the paint thickness and so was less likely to be pulled off by the flails of carriage washing plants. *Colin Boocock*

Above: The interior of a second-class section in the overhauled 'Brighton Belle' Pullman train shows the traditional layout and superb marquetry on the end wall wood panelling. The seats were trimmed with BR's standard blue moquette, which looked surprisingly attractive. *British Rail*

Right: To commemorate Eastleigh town's long association with railways, Class 33 No 33008 was named *Eastleigh* at a ceremony at the station on 11 April 1980. *Brian Morrison*

8. From BREL to BRML

At the creation of British Railways Workshops in 1962 the works ceased to be directly managed by the Southern Region. The next organisational change to come was the creation in 1973 of British Rail Engineering Limited, or BREL as it was colloquially and commercially known. The changes followed the desire to allow the workshops to compete in engineering markets and created a new structure with a corporate headquarters and its own managing director and board reporting to the British Railways Board.

In the 1970s, the BRB had formed a number of wholly owned subsidiary companies which were run at an arms-length relationship with the BRB, of which BREL was one. The long-term aim was to prepare these companies for possible future sale to the private sector. BREL continued the process of elimination of surplus workshop capacity, including the closure of several well-known large locomotive works including Darlington and Swindon.

By the early 1980s, the BRB realised that a huge slice of its costs came from the overhaul and maintenance of traction and rolling stock. Thus began the Manufacturing and Maintenance Policy Review which was completed in 1986. Works such as Eastleigh had traditionally undertaken complete overhauls of rolling stock in that, at a due date or condition, the vehicle was stripped and reassembled with new or overhauled components ready for service as a complete re-engineered unit. The policy review concluded that this was an inefficient approach because not all components were worn sufficiently to need replacement at the same time, and thus some were changed too early.

The review decided that British Rail should, where possible, decouple the overhaul intervals of mileage and hours-sensitive parts from calendar time-sensitive parts. Thus diesel engines should be changed on engine hours (or breakdown) in depots or workshops while transmissions and bogies should be changed on mileage, with a quick turnaround. Vehicle bodies would receive treatment at general or intermediate overhaul (locomotives) and C1, C2 or C6 attention (carriages) as their condition required.

New vehicle building, heavy overhaul and component repairs were to be put out to competitive tender. In 1988, British Rail Engineering Limited was divided into two companies: BREL (1988) Ltd which took on the four remaining major engineering works and British Rail Maintenance Limited (BRML). BRML comprised mostly the smaller works which were used for periodic maintenance of rolling stock including the sites at Glasgow, Wolverton, Doncaster and Eastleigh. Chart Leacon (Ashford), Ilford, Stratford and Swindon Electronic Services Centre were added to BRML later.

Business sectors

At about this time, BRB Chairman (Sir) Bob Reid was concerned that the only place in the whole railway system where revenue and costs came together and profit or loss could be calculated was at the top. In consequence, he introduced the main railway businesses, each of which would have its own 'bottom line' and profit and loss account. These new businesses were: InterCity, Provincial, London & South East, Freight and Parcels. Each of these had its own director and decisions emerged which would benefit the particular business sector.

London & South East under Chris Green's direction later became known as Network SouthEast (NSE). This business created a very strong visual image in traction and rolling stock and infrastructure and became the key customer for Eastleigh Works.

With its location in the South Western business sub-sector of Network SouthEast, Eastleigh Works was able to focus on the local rolling stock market, although as multiple-units gained sway on most services, the visits of locomotives for traditional overhauls became rarer.

Examples of rolling stock work undertaken at Eastleigh during this period included the refurbishment of former London Transport stock, introduced as part of the modernisation of the Isle of Wight railway in 1989-90. Nine two-car sets were formed from redundant 1938 tube stock, the vehicles being rebuilt at Eastleigh Works and shipped to the island. Also dealt with at this time was the refurbishment of traditional Southern Region stock such as the 4-VEP EMUs. The works fitted fluorescent lighting and updated interiors including the replacement of wooden tables by those made of glass-reinforced plastic (GRP). There was also the replacement of metal slam doors with GRP examples. For decades, the plastics shop had been a particular specialisation of Eastleigh, and produced parts right up to the end of 2005.

To upgrade the London Victoria to Gatwick Airport service, BR's basic philosophy was to use Class 73 electro-diesel locomotives as the main traction unit together with stock converted from Mk 2f air-conditioned coaches and driving luggage vans adapted from former 2-HAP EMU driving motor coaches. The work on the luggage vehicles was carried out at Eastleigh Works in late 1983 and early 1984. The body sides were extensively modified to provide three pairs of double doors spaced equally along the vehicle. The sides of the coach were also extended downwards over the solebars to provide a tumblehome to match that of the passenger coaches. At the inner end, a corridor connection and guard's compartment were fitted and removal of the passenger area provided significant luggage storage space. Mechanically the existing motor bogie was retained. New control desks were fitted in order to be able to provide remote control for the Class 73 locomotive at the opposite end of the train.

Eastleigh Works also undertook the conversion of the passenger vehicles which were built at Derby Carriage Works in 1973-74. These were coupled in semi-permanent formations of four and three cars and were bar-coupled together with high-level air and jumper connections fitted on the set ends. Handbrakes were fitted

Right: **New staging was put up by BREL in the former van shop for a production scheme to rebuild existing carriages for the new Gatwick Express service. The Class 489 driving motor luggage vans were converted from 2-HAP driving motor vehicles such as from unit No 6071 which was well under way on 13 May 1983. The passenger-carrying stock for the Gatwick Express services was modified from BR Mk 2f coaches.** *David Warwick*

Left: **As well as work on conventional vehicles, an unusual task for Eastleigh Works was the refurbishment of London Underground 1938 stock for the Isle of Wight. This is one of the converted units resplendent in the bright NSE livery, ready for transfer to the Island.** *BRML*

Above: **A completed Gatwick Express unit is seen at Gatwick Airport station. The driving motor luggage van has its powered bogie nearest the camera. The 500bhp provided by the two EE507 traction motors in this vehicle supplemented the electro-diesel locomotive's output to produce 2,100bhp for the train.** *Colin Boocock*

Right: **The Gatwick Express passenger-carrying vehicles were converted Mk 2fs, the work undertaken at Eastleigh Works where they were adapted to operate as fixed-formation units. After privatisation, Class 73/2 Bo-Bo electro-diesel No 73207 *County of East Sussex* heads past South Croydon with the 14.00 from London Victoria to Gatwick Airport on 13 May 1999. Prior to privatisation these locomotives and carriages were painted in standard BR InterCity colours.** *Colin Boocock*

and toilet accommodation was converted to give extra luggage space.

Eastleigh's workforce acted in a very flexible manner and the business awareness of the management culture made sure that suitable work was always being sought to keep the works busy. As examples, one could see in the works receiving attention EMUs and DMUs from north of the Thames, locomotive-hauled InterCity stock and even freight vehicles. There were also examples of *ad hoc* work on locomotives.

The need to stay in touch with the local town was also recognised. The works provided a flamboyant float at the local Eastleigh town carnivals and the works open days were a popular draw with their historical content, but also available for public view was the current workload on the site.

Left: On the carriage overhaul layout in the combined works a traditional compartment seat from an old suburban EMU receives attention from the sewing needle in the trimming shop. Seat parts can be seen in the background hanging from the continuous belt that delivered work to various sites around this shop. *BREL*

Right and below: **Eastleigh's 'bread-and-butter' work during the BREL and BRML years included overhaul and relivery work on 4-VEP electric units (Class 423). The first picture shows VEP motor coach No S62184 stripped of its slam doors and still sporting British Rail corporate blue-and-grey. Later, the complete unit, with driving trailer No 76889 to the fore, stands in the works yard, resplendent in the colourful Network SouthEast livery.** *BRML*

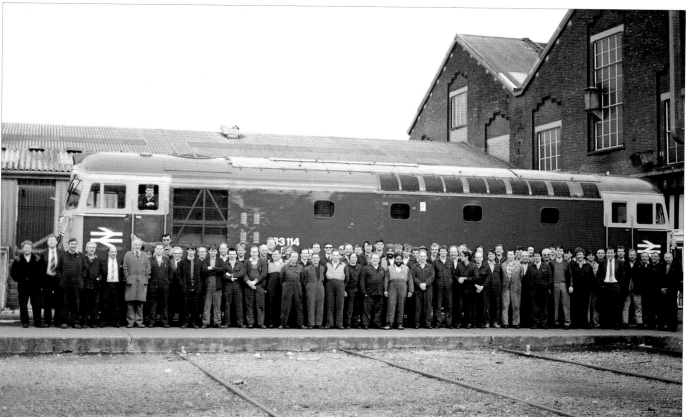

Top: **The works continued to develop its capability for electric traction machine repairs. In the electricians' shop in No 1 bay, traction motors are lined up for overhaul in August 1987.** *BRML*

Above: **BRML continued with locomotive overhaul work at Eastleigh and this was the last Class 33 to receive a classified repair there. No 33114 in BR rail blue livery is posed with the staff looking pleased with their product.** *BRML*

Left: **While work on LUL stock for the Isle of Wight goes on alongside in September 1989, an overhead crane carries a heavy spreader beam to lift out the Sulzer power unit from a BR Railfreight Class 47 Co-Co diesel-electric.** *BRML*

Above: **A feature of the work carried out for several decades at Eastleigh was the overhaul of power units from Southern DEMU vehicles. Work is in progress in the diesel shop on 4SRKT power units.** *BREL*

Right: **On the progressive carriage overhaul layout 4-VEP vehicle No S62184 receives additional work to body panelling in the guard's van area. In addition to refitting all the overhauled body parts on this layout, painters visited the vehicles on the last few stages to rub down and prepare the bodysides for spray painting, which was undertaken in the separate paint shop.** *BRML*

Left: As built, the 4-VEPs were supplied with small incandescent lamp bulbs to illuminate the passenger saloons and other areas. They also had heavy tubular-framed luggage racks across the cars located above the seat backs. BRML undertook a face-lift for some units at overhaul that replaced the old-fashioned lighting with more modern fluorescent tubes. This view also shows the more conventional side-wall luggage racks. *BRML*

Below: October 1990 saw a further expansion of the works' reach with the first of several Class 150 'Sprinter' DMUs overhauled and repainted. On the right is DMS No 57112 of unit No 150112 in the green-and-grey livery of the West Midlands Passenger Transport Executive. On the left is driving trailer vehicle No 76626 from Class 421 4-CIG unit No 1313. *Brian Morrison*

Right: The first Centro-liveried DMU, No 150202, received final attention on 22 November 1990 in the diesel test house after its overhaul, where it was accompanied by Bo-Bo diesel-electric No 33047 in the grey-and-yellow livery of BR's Central Services departmental fleet. *Brian Morrison*

Below right: BRML received some good publicity in the 1991 Eastleigh town carnival with its float showing a stylised Class 442 EMU with a steam locomotive at the other end of the tunnel! Eastleigh Works floats were a regular feature of town carnivals for many decades. *BRML*

Left: In August 1991, the Eastleigh Carnival Queen undertook charitable duties in the works. The staging for effective access to carriage bodies under overhaul is seen in the background. *BRML*

Below: Some works open days were the occasion to attract a range of locomotive exhibits of classes not normally seen at Eastleigh. This is the final Class 58 Co-Co diesel-electric parked outside the works offices for the September 1988 event. *BRML*

Right: To accommodate the longer carriages of the Class 442 'Wessex Express' EMUs, which are based on Mk 3 23m bodyshells, BRML reorganised the layout in two bays of the former erecting shop, including moving the paint shop from No 2 bay to No 1 bay. The programme of overhaul lifts for these EMUs was well under way in July 1991, as seen here. *BRML*

Below right: Eastleigh Works undertook some interesting conversion work as part of its policy of meeting its customers' requirements. Here, Bo-Bo diesel-electric No 33102 is with a rail scrubbing demonstration unit fitted to a former GUV vehicle numbered AM977695. They are standing in the yard of the diesel depot adjacent to the works, on 17 October 1991. *Brian Morrison*

Left: A notable feature of the works for many years was its variety of shunting locomotives. By BRML days the works had its own locomotive rather than having to use one supplied by the nearby diesel depot. This is the resident No 08642/D3809 in an attractive and possibly unique BRML lined black livery. It is accompanied by an adaptor wagon for moving multiple-unit vehicles around the yard. *BRML*

Below left: More modern EMUs began to appear at Eastleigh for overhaul in the early 1990s. Network SouthEast (NSE) livery is shown to advantage in the fresh finish on No 319104 in June 1992. *BRML*

Right: By using the traditional uroalkyd paints, carriages needed repainting every three or so years as a result of attack and deposits from carriage washing machines. In the paint shop, the NSE livery is reapplied to a 4-VEP unit by brush. The use of spray paint was possible, but the multi-colour livery would have been complicated to apply by this means. *BRML*

Below: Slam-door suburban units also received the NSE livery; 2-HAP unit No 5616 positively gleams in September 1992. It is standing in the yard after overhaul prior to being drawn forward onto the part of the exit track that was fitted with a conductor rail. All dc EMUs were driven directly from the works yard to Wimbledon depot for recommissioning after the third rail was fitted in the works yard from 1967. *BRML*

Above: When carriages were involved in a 'side swipe' collision, the damage to the body framing could be considerable and expensive to repair. In this example, a large area of lower body panelling has been removed from the VEP vehicle prior to the structural steel being cut out and replaced with new material. *BRML*

Right: Collision damage was a speciality of the works. This is the dismantled cab front of unit No 319049 that has been removed from the vehicle. *BRML*

Top right: Fortunately, most of the damage to No 319049 appears to have been superficial and confined to the glass-fibre cab front moulding which is relatively easy to repair. The vehicle is depicted awaiting reinstatement of the repaired cab front. *BRML*

Far right: The works did not confine itself to dc units. Here, BDTSO No 75471 from Class 305 25kV ac unit No 305410 receives attention in the erecting shop after repainting in NSE livery. One of its Gresley bogies is in the foreground. *Brian Morrison*

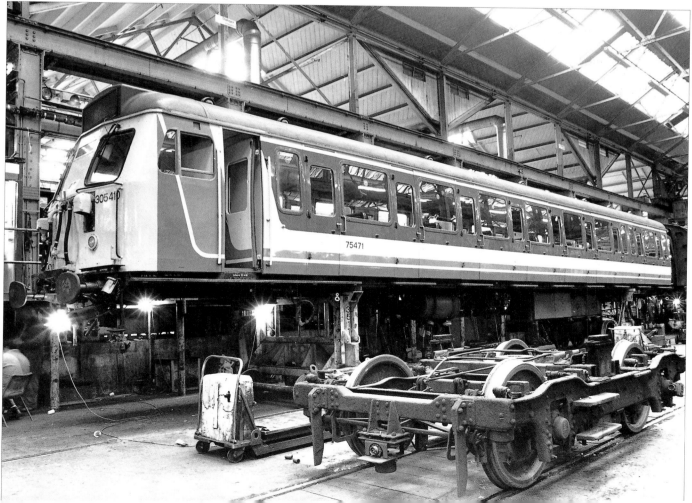

Right: Many BR businesses used Eastleigh Works to overhaul their equipment. Here is freshly repainted Parcels Sector Co-Co diesel-electric No 47709 ready to return to duty in August 1993. *BRML*

Left: The 455 dc EMUs were very familiar units at Eastleigh Works. These are two of the class ready to return to work with the NSE business sector. *BRML*

Right: The works continued to adapt to change and the workshops layout was modified as necessary. Here, we see a new pit being laid in the Class 442 EMU refurbishment bay in September 1993. *BRML*

Above: In February 1994 the works yard shows its final layout at the London end. Two water reservoirs are in the centre foreground and the single-track special repair shop for heavy body repairs is to the right. *BRML*

Below: A key speciality of the works was the production of GRP mouldings in the plastics shop. This is a classic Mk 1 slam door being laid up. *BRML*

Left: An expert craftsman is seen at work painting a coach from a Class 442 unit as it is prepared for its return to traffic. For complex liveries such as this NSE 'coat of many colours', the paint shop reverted to hand painting. *BRML*

Below: Several rakes of InterCity sector Mk 2 air-conditioned stock for the West Coast main line received the business's livery at Eastleigh. A freshly finished rake stands in the works yard in May 1997. *BRML*

9. The privatisation era

Above: **This panoramic composition shows Eastleigh Works in its last full year of operation, 2005. Additional buildings that are not present in earlier views in this book include: extreme left, the traction motor rewind shop which later became a stores; centre left, the heavy vehicle repair building that enabled collision and corrosion damage to be repaired before vehicles entered the overhaul layout in the works; and right (behind the two Class 73/2 locomotives), the component cleaning shop which used high-pressure water jets to clean components before overhaul. Only three months later the yard was virtually clear of all railway vehicles as the works was run down before final closure.** *Colin Boocock*

The formation of BRML had changed the way the smaller works operated and had taken most of them away from the traditional heavy overhauls. As privatisation began, BR set up a detailed process of sales and tendering and eventually Eastleigh Works entered the private sector as Wessex Traincare Ltd via a management buyout made on 7 June 1995. Other parts of BRML were sold direct to ABB, Babcock and Siemens. This then precipitated a period of ownership changes. In February 1998, GEC-Alsthom bought Wessex Traincare which at the time had annual sales of £42 million. Changes continued and in December 1998 Alstom (as the company was now known) announced 300 redundancies at Eastleigh.

A key reason for the almost continuous reduction in workload, both during the BR era as well as the privatised era, was the introduction of trains that needed overhaul far less frequently. An example is that a Class 455 EMU runs at least twice the mileage between lifts for bogie overhauls than did a conventional BR Mk 1 unit such as a 4-EPB. Probably the final nail in Eastleigh's coffin was the failure of Alstom to gain the new-build contract for trains to replace South West Trains' slam-door stock, and the consequent opening by the successful bidder, Siemens, of its new depot at Northam which incorporated bogie-change facilities. A further reduction of workload came from the ability to cheaply relivery vehicles at depots with vinyls, and the fitment of seat and floor coverings that can be changed at depots rather than needing works attention.

In mid-December 2004, Alstom announced that it was going to close its Eastleigh renovation plant with the loss of some 530 jobs.

The last major vehicle work programme at Eastleigh was the refurbishment of electric multiple-units from the Southern and Merseyrail train operators. Eastleigh had, for some years, also covered general repairs to Freightliner wagons; this was done in the former container shop.

Work at Eastleigh on Class 508 EMUs included sets refurbished for Connex South Eastern in 1998. The larger part of the work, however, concentrated on the Class 507/508 refurbishing for Merseyrail, giving passenger accommodation improvements including upgraded interiors along with engineering enhancement to improve performance. The final unit to undergo refurbishment was in the works in July 2005.

Alstom-built Gatwick Express units of Class 460 also visited the works in 2005 for C4 overhaul but the final chapter at Eastleigh Works, however, was seen out by the Class 455 refurbishment project for Southern which ran on at the works through until 2006. These units were extensively refurbished with bodywork treated to remove corrosion and new vinyl-covered floors were fitted. The low-backed seats were replaced with high-backed versions and spaces for wheelchairs created. All interior finishes were replaced and CCTV cameras installed, windows were replaced with vandal-resistant glass and a modern passenger information system fitted. The most noticeable exterior difference was the removal of the end gangways, which were plated over and made draught-proof. However, the last EMU to be overhauled at Eastleigh was an SWT Class 455 unit.

Late 2005 saw the appearance of advertisements for the auction of the works machinery and gradually items started to disappear from the works yard as they were sold or cut up for scrap. In its last years, Eastleigh Works yard was shunted by Class 08 0-6-0 diesel-electric No 08649 *G. H. Stratton* which was in a unique Alstom livery.

Inside the works, steam traction still had a presence with the preserved 4-6-0 No 850 *Lord Nelson* undergoing restoration by a private team on behalf of its owner, the National Railway Museum. Two ex-Gatwick Express Class 73/2s, which had stood in the works for some time, were taken away for preservation and a new lease of life towards the end of the year, while a locomotive which was maintained by the Eastleigh Railway Preservation Society remained on site until the following year. This was a former Southampton Docks 0-6-0 diesel-electric Class 07 shunter and it is likely that this humble machine will carry the accolade of being the last locomotive to grace the tracks of what we all used to know as Eastleigh Locomotive Works.

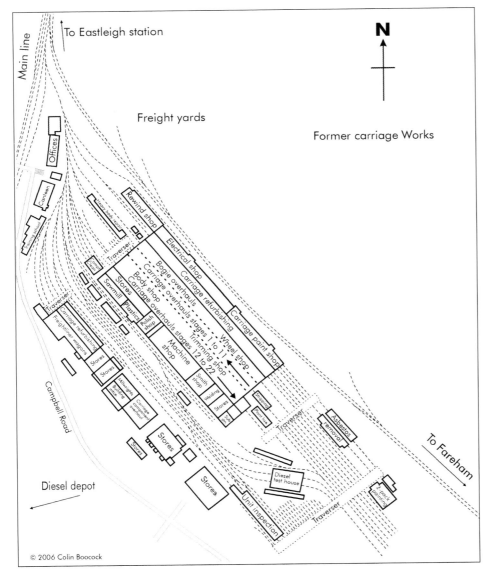

Left:
Figure 6: Eastleigh Works post 1996.

Top right: **After privatisation of BR, the train leasing companies and operators set up important programmes for refurbishing and life-extending their trains. Eastleigh Works adapted well to this type of work, as seen from this selection of dc EMUs in the works on 19 July 2005. Class 455 vehicles from both the South West Trains and Southern franchises are receiving attention on the high mobile stands in this view, while bogie frames wait for cleaning and overhaul on the adjacent track. The right-hand side of the high staging had been dismantled as it was not needed following the near-elimination of slam-door stock from the workload at Eastleigh.**
Colin Boocock

Right: **A Southern Class 455 EMU in the livery of the former Connex franchise enters the progressive layout staging for heavy refurbishment. The vehicle interior is being stripped in preparation for the replacement of fittings, and awaits lifting on 19 July 2005.**
Colin Boocock

Left: A major contract was undertaken at Eastleigh for the Angel Trains leasing company to overhaul the Merseyrail fleet of Class 507 and 508 EMUs. A vehicle of the last unit of the contract is seen here almost complete on the heavy side of the stage layout on 19 July 2005. Sadly, the usual enthusiasm for tidiness tends to dissipate when a factory is facing closure, as was Eastleigh at this time. *Colin Boocock*

Above: The result of Eastleigh Works' refurbishment of the Merseyrail EMUs is illustrated in this view of unit No 507026 coming to a stand at Garston station on 10 November 2005. Apart from a complete livery change, the end lamp clusters had been revised fully to meet Railway Group Standards requirements including the 'triangle of lights' arrangement. Internally, the trains have been given higher-backed seating, modern information displays and better accommodation for disabled passengers. *Colin Boocock*

Below:
Vehicles receiving lift attention in No 4 bay were still lifted off their bogies at Stage 3 and placed on high movable stands for easy access to underfloor equipment. The staging had been removed on one side for easier access. *Colin Boocock*

Above: **To provide extra shop space to enable the works to overhaul the 23m long vehicles of Class 442, the paint shop was moved from No 2 bay to No 1 bay. In the paint shop this Southern Class 455 vehicle has received dark green undercoat. A painter is rubbing down filler to smooth the surface before application of the final two-pack gloss-paint colours. This was done in a sealed building in the works yard.** *Colin Boocock*

Below: **Final touches are being applied to the main colours on two refurbished Southern class 455 carriages. The contrasting colours around the passenger access doors meet the disabled access requirements for visibility.** *Colin Boocock*

Above: This Class 455 unit has received its final coat of colours for the Southern train operating company on 19 July 2005. The traverser in the foreground enabled movement of vehicles from one track to another within the confines of the shop to support progressive working. *Colin Boocock*

Below: On 6 June 2005, Southern Class 455 EMU No 455846 was at London Bridge station on the 12.41 London Charing Cross to Tattenham Corner service. The refurbishing of these units at Eastleigh has brought their interiors close to the standard of the new Electrostar trains used on Southern's main line services. *Colin Boocock*

Above: In the late 1990s it became possible to relivery a carriage by applying vinyl stickers to the bodysides. An early example was the advertising livery carried by selected Gatwick Express Mk 2 coaches. This practice soon enabled depots to relivery complete trains and reduced their dependence on main works for this work, thus taking another step towards reduction in the need for facilities such as that at Eastleigh. This is the 15.05 to London Victoria awaiting departure from Gatwick Airport station on 18 October 2000. *Colin Boocock*

Below: Modern Alstom traction rests in No 2 bay on 19 July 2005. Half of a Class 460 Gatwick Express EMU sits on stands awaiting placement on its overhauled bogies. These vehicles had been delivered new from Alstom painted with two-pack paints that could last upwards of eight years. This is another nationwide practice that has substantially reduced the need to send trains to main works for body overhauls. *Colin Boocock*

Above: **Freshly overhauled bogies in No 3 bay await installation under a Gatwick Express Class 460 unit on 19 July 2005. The bogie frame washing facility on the left was colloquially known as the 'bogie bosh'.** *Colin Boocock*

Below: **In this general view of the wheel shop at Eastleigh works on 19 July 2005 protection rails have been erected to prevent damage to wheelset journals and bearings from internal vehicles works passing by. On the right is a blue-painted mechanical auger which removes metal swarf (turnings) from the adjacent wheel profiling machine, for deposit in a large bin.** *Colin Boocock*

Above: **Before Royal Mail opted out of the general use of rail transport some of the EWS-owned NFX vans were rebuilt at Eastleigh Works as type NBA for such traffic. These are Nos 94543 and 94544 in the works yard on 6 November 2001.** *Brian Morrison*

Below: **A significant contract in the closing years of the works was the general overhaul of Freightliner wagons. This is the main frame of an overhauled wagon in No 4 bay on 19 July 2005. A complete bogie overhaul was dealt with in an adjacent shop while other work on these wagons was done in the former van shop (once the iron foundry).** *Colin Boocock*

Right: **Overhaul of Freightliner wagon frames and bogies continued apace in the former iron foundry until the works closed.** *Colin Boocock*

Left: **The adjacent bay still contains the staging erected to facilitate the conversion of Mk 2f vehicles for the Gatwick Express sets, although by 2005 lack of this type of work rendered the capacity surplus. The design of the staging incorporated side flaps which could be lifted for access to equipment under the vehicle solebar.** *Colin Boocock*

Below: **These two test houses were provided to facilitate final assembly and preparation of multiple-units for traffic. Each contained a pitted track and enabled what in the 1970s had been a cold and wet outdoor job to be undertaken in more comfortable conditions.** *Colin Boocock*

Above: **Back in BREL and BRML days, Eastleigh Works was faced with BR's programme for the elimination of asbestos from carriages. Blue asbestos had been used as heat and sound insulation on large numbers of BR Mk 1 vehicles, sprayed on internal bodysides with white asbestos sheets placed under floors. The asbestos-removal buildings at Eastleigh were built at different times between 1970 and 1982 at the far south-eastern end of the works yard, a sensible environmental** judgement. **Following completion of this programme, one of the buildings was converted to a facility for spraying carriages with two-pack paint. This is how the shops looked on 19 July 2005.** *Colin Boocock*

Below: **In comparison with the steam era, the heavy capacity of the works was much reduced but the capability to tackle some key tasks was retained. The smith shop even continued with one of its older, air-operated hammers.** *Peter Stanton*

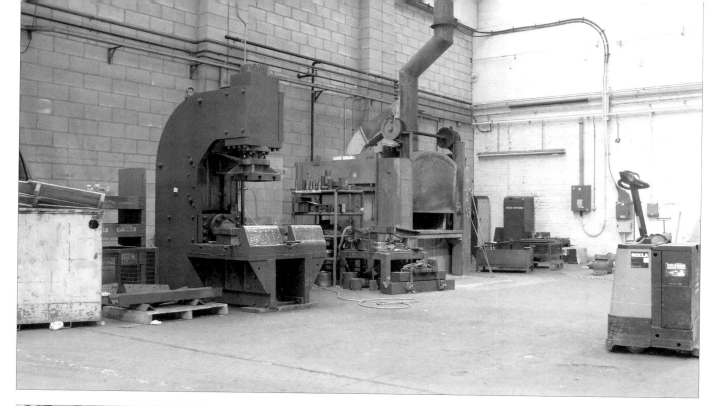

Top: The smith shop also benefited from the use of a modern hammer but there was a need for an updated version of a traditional hearth alongside. The concrete floor had become standard for all changes to the infrastructure of the works undertaken since the 1962 Workshops Plan was begun. *Colin Boocock*

Above: By the time of this view of the machine shop in July 2005, many machines had been computer-controlled for several years. A significant machining capacity had been retained, but the area was to become empty after the closing-down auction held in September 2005. *Colin Boocock*

Above: Large factories can survive only if their stores organisations are effective. At Eastleigh there were several stores buildings strategically sited near the facilities they served. This one was a late addition, located in the former rewind building outside No 1 bay. *Colin Boocock*

Below: Mobile plant was another valuable asset on which the works could call to shift heavy materials between the stores and the shops. This mobile road crane sits outside the main stores in July 2005 having performed its last duties. It awaits disposal by auction. *Peter Stanton*

Top: By 2005 the plastics shop occupied a smaller area but still produced a significant output of parts as well as carrying out repairs to existing plastic components. *Colin Boocock*

Above: Class 455 vehicle No 71731 stands beyond the traverser at the north-west end of the shops on 19 July 2005. This carriage had been used to experiment with external plug doors and subsequently became a demonstrator for the South West Trains EMU refurbishment programme. It was cut up at Eastleigh Works on 5 October 2005. *Colin Boocock*

Left: **On 17 May 2006, the preserved 4-6-0 steam locomotive No 850 *Lord Nelson*, an item in the National Collection, was steamed at Eastleigh Works following its overhaul to make it fit for further main line running. This overhaul was undertaken by private volunteers, members of the Eastleigh Railway Preservation Society, within the premises of Eastleigh Works.** *Colin Boocock*

Below: **The works offices remained in use right through to 2006 and this view in June shows clearly the rectangular extension that was added at the London end as part of the 1962 BR Workshops Plan. Such a clash in architectural styles would probably not have been countenanced in more recent years.** *Colin Boocock*

Right: **This general view, taken on 19 July 2005, shows the relationship of Eastleigh Works (in the background) with the station approach infrastructure. A pair of Siemens Desiro Class 444 express electric units heads round the curve on to the Portsmouth line, while a Bombardier Class 170 DMU arrives on the Totton–Romsey shuttle. With the exception of the unpopular Class 458 units in the London area, by summer 2005** South West Trains was operating no Alstom-built trains and virtually all the slam-door stock had gone. Siemens was successful in obtaining the contract to replace almost all SWT's slam-door stock with units from its Desiro range, this sounding the death-knell of Alstom's Eastleigh Works. The company finally pulled out of train maintenance activity there on **31 March 2006.** *Colin Boocock*

Above: **Many types of locomotive were used over the years as works shunting locomotives. First, there were the old LSWR Beyer Peacock-type 0-6-0STs, then we recall in particular the Class 0395 0-6-0s that held sway from the 1920s through to the 1950s, then the two PD&SWJR 0-6-2Ts, and latterly various Class 08 0-6-0 diesel-electrics.**

This photograph shows what was the last official works shunter at Eastleigh, No 08649, decked out in Alstom livery as No D3816. It carried the nameplate *G. H. Stratton.* The diamond-shaped decorative plate on the cabside showed a Spitfire aeroplane; the design of this plate was used for BR Railfreight locomotives operating out of Eastleigh depot in recognition that the neighbouring airfield, now Southampton Airport, was an early base for World War 2 test flights of these famous fighter aircraft. *Colin Boocock*

Index

Right: **The very last overhauled EMU, South West Trains Class 455 No 5918, is hauled out through the works gate** *en route* **to Wimbledon depot at the end of March 2006.** *Nigel Guppy*

Below: **Sadly, the last few years of Alstom's operations in Eastleigh Works saw the workload contracting severely and the works yard was becoming visually desolate in July 2005. Two Class 73/2 electro-diesels, Nos 73210 and 73211, released from their Gatwick Express duties by the delivery of Alstom Class 460 Juniper EMUs, stand forlorn near the shed used for pressure cleaning of used components.** *Colin Boocock*

Above: **The enevitable emptiness after closure of the works. Eastleigh's No 4 Bay on 12th June 2006 looks stripped clean. What is its future now?**